VISUALIZE YOUR GREATNESS

MIKE SINGLETARY
WITH GORDON DASHER

VISUALIZE YOUR GREATNESS

THE PLAYBOOK FOR **THE SEVEN Cs OF SUCCESS**

Copyright © 2025 by Mike Singletary.

All rights reserved. No part of this book may be used or reproduced in any manner whatsoever without prior written consent of the author, except as provided by the United States of America copyright law.

Published by Advantage Books, Charleston, South Carolina.
An imprint of Advantage Media.

ADVANTAGE is a registered trademark, and the Advantage colophon is a trademark of Advantage Media Group, Inc.

Printed in the United States of America.

10 9 8 7 6 5 4 3 2 1

ISBN: 979-8-89188-333-8 (Paperback)
ISBN: 979-8-89188-334-5 (eBook)

Library of Congress Control Number: 2025909590

Cover design by David Taylor.
Layout design by Ruthie Wood.

This publication is designed to provide accurate and authoritative information in regard to the subject matter covered. It is sold with the understanding that the publisher is not engaged in rendering legal, accounting, or other professional services. If legal advice or other expert assistance is required, the services of a competent professional person should be sought.

Advantage Books is an imprint of Advantage Media Group. Advantage Media helps busy entrepreneurs, CEOs, and leaders write and publish a book to grow their business and become the authority in their field. Advantage authors comprise an exclusive community of industry professionals, idea-makers, and thought leaders. For more information go to **advantagemedia.com**.

✕ ✕ ✕ ✕

CONTENTS

FOREWORD IX

AUTHOR'S NOTE XIII

INTRODUCTION. 1

PRINCIPLE 1 17
COURAGE

PRINCIPLE 2 37
CONSCIOUSNESS

PRINCIPLE 3 63
CONSISTENCY

PRINCIPLE 4 85
CONFIDENT

PRINCIPLE 5 103
CHARACTER

PRINCIPLE 6 131
COMPETE

PRINCIPLE 7 169
COMMITTED

EPILOGUE 205

ACKNOWLEDGEMENTS 211

FOREWORD

As a kid growing up in West Texas, I loved playing baseball, and was blessed to even play it professionally in the minor leagues. But my real calling was in medicine, which allowed me to make a difference in people's lives. It also allowed me to meet Mike Singletary.

I was blessed with a long and successful medical career that allowed me to become a professor and founding chairman of the Department of Neurological Surgery at Northwestern University's Feinberg School of Medicine in Chicago.

In 2010, society was grappling with disturbing headlines that stated some former NFL players were being diagnosed during autopsy with chronic traumatic encephalopathy. The NFL was under great pressure to report what was going on. Commissioner Goodell recruited Dr. Richard Ellenbogen and me to cochair the new NFL Head, Neck, and Spine Committee. As a committee, we were tasked with designing a strategy for the on-field diagnosis of concussion and subsequent return-to-play guidelines. In addition, we had access to emerging technologies for helmets and other protective equipment. Alongside the NFL Competition Committee, we developed rules that expanded the definition of a defenseless player. In addition, by advancing the restraining line on kickoffs, we reduced concussions on kickoffs by 40 percent. This was important and interesting work, and we learned a lot from it, but it is fair to say that one of the most impactful aspects of that part of my life was the relationship I formed with Mike Singletary.

Mike contacted me after my return to Dallas and the University of Texas Southwestern Medical Center as chair of neurosurgery. As a Hall of Fame middle linebacker and one who had played with ferocity, he knew what it meant to make a hard tackle. He had cracked twelve helmets in college and numerous others with the Chicago Bears, yet he had never sustained a concussion. That was remarkable to me. As a baseball and basketball player, I had experienced at least six concussions. The answer to that dichotomy became obvious. Mike's technique of tackling with his head up so he could see what he was hitting and then driving his shoulder through the opponent's belly button was not only incredibly effective but also highly protective. Because of his small size and the advice he received from a coach early in high school, Mike worked to develop incredible strength and musculature in his neck. But as powerful as his neck is, the most impressive part of Mike is his heart.

He initially reached out to me because of his concern for many former NFL players, some of whom had suffered tragic consequences from their playing careers. He told me about one conversation he'd had with former defensive lineman Lyle Alzado, who approached Mike during a Pro Bowl event and said that, at age forty-two, he was considering trying to go back to professional football. Six months later, he was dead. Mike internalized many of those stories and the lives they affected in a deep way. He and his son John came to my office to record a conversation about concussions and what was happening with former athletes. Too many of Mike's friends were not doing well. Mike told me how he would convene a meeting each year at the Hall of Fame event in Canton, Ohio. Too many times, he told me, legends of the game and his idols would come up to him to ask a question. They would ask the same question again and again and then struggle to find their way back to their seats. "We have to find the answer to this," he told me.

How could a small, frail child growing up in an underprivileged neighborhood with ten siblings and a violent father become the Mike Singletary we all know? His story of painful experiences was channeled into a life that surpassed any idea of what should have been possible. Through my role with the NFL and Mike's desire to help others, Mike and I traveled the country together and spoke to many diverse audiences regarding ways to prevent these injuries and protect athletes from childhood to adulthood. You have no idea how many times we were asked, "Should I let my son play football?" or "Should I let my daughter play lacrosse?" Throughout that process, we developed a friendship and then, one night, I suffered a fall related to atrial fibrillation and a medication I was on, resulting in two emergency spinal operations and extensive rehabilitation. Throughout my time in the hospital, we restricted my visitors to the neurosurgery residents, my family, Merry Quinson, Scott Clamp, and Mike Singletary. Mike would come to see me at night. I was trying to learn to walk again, and I was very weak in my left leg. Mike would coach me about envisioning the movements that I needed to make and then trusting my leg as I shifted my weight into it. "Envision the play," he told me, "then trust it and execute it."

In some ways, this is how Mike saved himself. When he was twelve years old, his mother, who prayed for him every day, told him that she recognized greatness within him and issued him a challenge. His response was to write an eight-point strategic plan for his life. The plan included getting a college scholarship, graduating, being an all-American, being drafted into the NFL, and ultimately playing in a Super Bowl. He did all that and much more. After my rehabilitation, we were meeting in my study, and I remember him saying, "Trust yourself; you have another chapter left." He was correct, and because I know firsthand, I can tell you that if you follow the advice he lays out in this monograph, your story will be better than you can imagine. Understanding Mike's incredible journey will empower you to overcome severe adversity, achieve the unimaginable, and, perhaps, save your own life. Mike has impacted me emotionally and spiritually. I know his story will do the same for you. Good luck, and God bless.

Hunt Batjer, MD

AUTHOR'S NOTE

Sometimes, someone will ask me about my childhood. I'm not going to lie—my younger days growing up in the rough-and-tumble Sunnyside community in South Houston were often difficult.

But as broken as Sunnyside was in those days, it wasn't the most broken neighborhood in Houston. Many of our neighbors owned their own homes. Some of the residents of Sunnyside prided themselves on keeping their houses painted and their yards cleaned and manicured. Most of our mothers and fathers, including my own, worked like dogs to make ends meet.

Still, when I think about my childhood, a certain sadness sometimes comes over me. Those were some hard times, to be sure. But if I'm being honest, some good memories manage to sneak through once in a while too. It wasn't all bad.

THE FAMILY BUSINESS, HARD WORK, AND INA'S DINER

My father owned a construction business that specialized in building decks and pouring driveways and patios. The truth is that he would take on almost any job he could in order to make a few bucks. He

VISUALIZE YOUR GREATNESS

was a flawed man, perhaps more flawed than most, but no one would ever say that my father didn't work hard.

Most of the folks in our neighborhood couldn't afford an outside contractor to build their decks or remodel their houses. If they needed something like that done, they did it themselves. As a result, the majority of my dad's jobs were in the more affluent areas of Houston.

So, every day Dad would load up his tools in the bed of his old pickup truck and head out to work on the other side of town.

I wish I could tell you the make and model of that truck, but I can't. In fact, I'm not sure it would actually be classified as one specific make or model at all. Back in the day, we used to call old worn-out cars *clunkers*. This truck was far below clunker status.

He didn't pay much for it, just a few bucks. The engine was shot, as well as the transmission. It was missing doors, and the bed was rotted through. Truthfully, it should have stayed in the junkyard.

My father not only worked hard, but he was resourceful too. Someone towed the truck for my father and parked it in our backyard. My dad then began to scour the junkyards for parts that he could scavenge to make the truck more useful. He paid no attention to whether the parts were from a Ford, a Dodge, or a Chevy—he usually found a way to make them work.

I wish I had a photo of that old jalopy of a truck. It was a hideous thing to behold. I do recall that Dad tinkered with it almost every day to keep it running. It was a work in progress—always a work in progress.

His personal vehicle, however, the one the family rode around in, was a Cadillac convertible that he had completely restored from the ground up. Dad repaired or replaced all the broken or worn-out parts and sanded and painted it himself. By the time he rolled that old Cadillac out on the streets of Sunnyside, it looked like a brand-new

AUTHOR'S NOTE

car. The Singletary family, all of us, would squeeze our hot bodies into the plush seats of that old Caddy and motor up and down the streets like we were all somebody.

But the truck? Now that was another matter. But Dad didn't care, and neither did we, because it served its purpose—it was just transportation, a tool to get a job done.

While many kids my age saw Saturday mornings and the summer break from school as a time to relax, I enjoyed no such luxury. My dad's business was a family business, so my brothers and I were expected to do our part.

It must have been a sight to behold when the Singletary boys, their cousins Ricky and Clintel, and my dad's brother, Uncle John, left Sunnyside and drove through Bellaire or one of the other "nicer" communities on our way to a job. With my older brothers and cousins lodged in between the tools and wheelbarrows and cement mixers in the bed of the truck, my dad behind the wheel, and my Uncle John on the passenger side of the cab, we were quite the spectacle.

And there I was, little Mike, right between my dad and Uncle John, with the manual transmission shifter sticking up between my knees. Every time Dad needed to shift gears, I had to move my leg to one side or the other to allow Dad enough room to do so.

We worked hard in those days. If you don't know much about the climate of Houston, Texas, the best way I can describe the summers there is to tell you that it's not that much different from being in a sauna. The heat is oppressive. It hovers like a blanket over South Texas and combines with an equally oppressive humidity. It is relentless! And it sucks the air from a person's lungs. From one day to the next, and on into the nights, summers in Houston never let up. They seem intent on beating a working man down to the ground.

As soon as the old truck rumbled to a stop and we began our labor, this blanket of heat wrapped a little tighter around our bodies, and our skin began to try to cool our core with sweat. I'm grateful now that God made people with a built-in cooling system, but when we were laboring in the hot air of Houston, the sweat was like a magnet for grit and sand. By the end of the day, when we loaded back up in Dad's old truck, we were one sweaty, dirty, smelly throng of men.

However, one good thing about quitting time is that we were all ready for a good meal and some cool air, and my brothers knew just where to go.

I wouldn't call my brothers sneaky, but they were crafty. Normally, when my father was working, he was in his element. Working and making a living made him happy. But every now and then, we noticed, for whatever reason, that he was in a foul mood. When that happened, we learned to keep our thoughts to ourselves. We did not dare to ask him for anything.

But at the end of most workdays, he was happy, almost jovial. My older brothers knew how to read my father. But, even on the good days, they were still afraid to ask him if we could stop at Ina's Diner on the way home. So, they recruited me, the youngest of the Singletary brothers, to formally present the request to our father.

Sneaky? I prefer to think of them as wise. They knew that since I was the baby of the family, I had a special relationship with our father. If I asked, they knew they stood a better chance of Dad saying yes.

Dad always knew that they had put me up to it, and he would usually grin slyly and respond with something like, "So, your brothers want to stop at Ina's, do they? Well, tell them to pack up the tools, and let's get on our way."

To be honest, I don't think it was a hard sell with Dad. Besides the great food at Ina's, there was the air-conditioning. I'll never forget

AUTHOR'S NOTE

that blast of cold air that hit me as soon as I walked through the door. Almost every building in Houston is air-conditioned now, but in the 1960s, it was a rare thing. We certainly didn't have it in our home.

Ina's was more than a place that served great food and afforded our sweaty bodies a few moments of cool comfort, however. It was also a place of community where many of the other patrons knew us. As soon as we shuffled our tired feet through the door, someone would yell out, "Well, here come the Singletary boys." Then the good-natured banter would begin.

My dad was a Pentecostal pastor, and they would start right in on him. "Hey, Rev. You and your boys don't eat all the food. Save some for us other working people." They would all have a good laugh, and my brothers would head for the jukebox and play Otis Redding, Sam Cooke, Marvin Gaye, or Stevie Wonder.

It was a little slice of heaven.

People liked to watch the Singletary boys eat. My brothers could really throw it down. As soon as the food hit the table, it disappeared. We hungrily gulped down Ina's tasty home cooking, sipped her ice-cold tea, and continued to joke among ourselves and the other patrons. We caught up on community news. I listened as the adult men talked about the state of our city and country.

Ina's was a successful Black-owned business that served as a meeting place for other Black business owners. People who cut trees, replaced roofs, laid brick, or poured concrete like our family did would gather at diners like Ina's.

These entrepreneurs met to compare notes and share tips about where the next big construction projects were going to be built. More than once, I heard one of these men tell the others, "There's a new subdivision going in at such and such a place. I sure could use some help."

Even though there were plenty of successful Black men and women in Houston back in the day, there was always an undercurrent of racial injustice in the air. I sometimes wondered, *Why are we limited to hard labor? Why can't we be doctors and lawyers and own businesses that also cater to Whites?*

Our time at Ina's was a small window where we could momentarily forget all of that.

The blessing of Ina's Diner to me is that the moments we spent there kindled a spark of desire in me. It was times like those, when the troubles of my life seemed to take a breather for a moment, that I asked myself, *Why can't I live like this all the time? Why are Ina's Diner and the barber shop the only places where I can be myself and have a good time? Why is church the only place I can dress up and go wearing my best clothes?*

THE MOOD OF SUNNYSIDE

While there were good times in Sunnyside back when I was a young boy, if you were to ask me to summarize the overall mood of my childhood neighborhood in one word, I would say that it was hopelessness.

I suppose that anyone looking at our community from the outside could make a judgment that we were lazy, that we didn't want to hope. That's an easy thing to say unless you were legally forced to live in segregated neighborhoods such as Sunnyside.

Our community was platted in the early 1900s by the city fathers for the specific purpose of creating a Black community that was geographically separated from other communities. It was annexed into Houston a couple of years before I was born, but even though we paid taxes, we received no city services—no sewer, water, or drainage.

AUTHOR'S NOTE

Yes, most people in Sunnyside had given up hope, but they had not given up hope because they were bad or lazy people. Hundreds of years before any of us were born, a lie was spoken about people like us: "You don't matter. At least, you don't matter as much as other people do."

This lie came from outside of Sunnyside—there's no denying that. But as bad as the lie coming in from the outside was, it was the way the lie was believed and repeated inside the community that did the most damage.

I don't think anyone I knew actually believed that they were less valuable than anyone else, but they did believe that the people who held power would never give them a fair shot at a better life. They felt trapped. As a result, many African Americans learned to see themselves as victims.

And that is the worst thing of all—a feeling of powerlessness. Victimhood breeds a hatred for initiative. It kills dreams and visions. It robs grown men of their dignity and reduces them to boys, or worse.

This was the thought, the idea that hung over Sunnyside and defined everything. In a sense, I get it. Black people in America were enslaved as mere property for longer than we have been emancipated. And by the 1950s, when I was born, many Black people still felt enslaved by the system.

I was born fewer than a hundred years after the Thirteenth Amendment was ratified, finally releasing the stronghold that slave owners had over their "property." By the time I came on the scene, the iron chains were gone. African American people who could trace their family roots to slavery were technically free. But everywhere we looked, there were signs (some literal, some unspoken and unwritten) that told us, "Yeah, about that freedom thing—not so fast."

VISUALIZE YOUR GREATNESS

Though the iron chains that bound the feet and wrists of African Americans were gone, many of us were still bound by the trauma of slavery, partly because the story was handed down from one generation to the next like it was a part of our DNA. Sadly, everything around us reinforced that trauma—the signs, the laws, the looks of disdain we felt from non-Black people.

This story still haunts us today. Many Black people work hard to remove the reminders of slavery by tearing down historical statues, and some Black athletes kneel at the playing of the national anthem in protest of our country's racist past.

Yet, the nagging trauma remains. In fact, the more we focus on these external symbols that represent the wrong that was done to us, the worse off we are. And the worse we think we are, the angrier we become. In many segments of Black communities, this anger is seething, boiling over into fits of rage.

The problem is, however, that we often don't really know who it is we are supposed to be angry with. Is it the police? The government? White people? Other Black people? The church? Our teachers? Our fathers? Ourselves?

We're just angry. And after all the outward expressions of anger, after we have torn down statues and dismantled institutions such as education, the church, and the government, we're still mad. And even if we were to be convinced that the pathway to real freedom runs through our forgiveness of those who've made life miserable for us, we don't really know who we're supposed to forgive because we don't know who we're actually angry at.

This is a vicious cycle. It is a special kind of slavery, an emotional and spiritual chain that, instead of restraining our movement by binding our feet and wrists, is wrapped tightly around our hearts and minds. These invisible chains restrain our upward movement toward greatness and excellence. We are still enslaved until we can figure out a way to release the anger in our hearts and the fear in our minds that drives our emotional dysfunction.

BROKEN PROMISES

A major part of this story is that, because of so many unkept promises by the government, some are still waiting for "the man" to come in and deliver us, to bring us our "stuff."

I'll admit that people in government have made too many unkept promises over the years to count. However, someone once said that the definition of insanity is when we keep on doing the same thing over and over and expecting different results. So, what do you call it when, after all these years have passed and after all of the broken promises, we are still waiting for the government to make things right for us?

What I say next may seem insensitive and cruel at first. But in reality, it is the kindest, most liberating thing I can say to anyone who still holds out hope that someone is coming to help us—*it ain't gonna happen!* There's no such thing as free stuff. At this point in the game, the only person who can liberate the person who feels enslaved is the person who feels enslaved.

HOW DO WE GET OUT OF THE MUD BOG OF DESPAIR?

Someone may ask, "So, how do we do that?"

That's a very good question. All I can do is tell my story of how I became liberated in my mind from the trap of victimhood. When I grew weary of being a casualty of my circumstances, I didn't look to the left or the right for another man to set me free. Instead, I looked upward to the only one who can actually free us—I sought out the God of creation.

The reason I went to him and him alone was that I was convinced he was the only one who could release me from the self-pity that was holding me back. I heard the message of God that promised me that I was capable of great things, and I wanted him to guide me from that point forward.

I am telling my story from the perspective of a Black man raised in an oppressive culture. But my assessment of what holds people back is universal. So is the solution to hopelessness. With God, it doesn't matter what color you are, what your daddy's last name is, where you live, or how rich or poor you are.

What really matters isn't *who* we are at all but *whose* we are. What matters is whom I belong to. When I discard the superficial identities that divide people into special classes and instead live life being fully aware that my life has been bought and paid for by the blood of Christ, I can live knowing that something special lies within me. I can now exercise my gifts. I can now follow my calling, a calling that has my name on it.

This is why I don't want anyone to give me anything. My mother always told me, "You don't want anything for free, because if they give it to you, they can always take it away. You only want the things you pay for or things you earn. There is only one gift you want for free, son, and that's the one that is already paid for—the gift of the blood of Jesus."

As I've thought about these things over the years, I'm convinced now, more than ever, that she was right. She didn't ignore the ugly legacy of slavery or institutional racism. She just knew that she didn't want her son to wait until the system changed before he could cast a vision for his life that would elevate him out of the attitudes of the

AUTHOR'S NOTE

hood that had him defeated before he even got started. She didn't want him to wait until someone somewhere else gave him permission to succeed.

Anything less is nothing more than another chain to bind our hearts and minds and to steal our dignity.

If we want to see how deadly this "we are waiting for someone else to do something for us" mindset is, all we have to do is look inside any community where it lives. There, we see crime, addiction to drugs and alcohol, the birth rate of children to unwed mothers, the absence of fathers, and living on a diet that is high in sugar and calories and low on actual nutrition.

This isn't unique to the Black community, but it's worth mentioning. African Americans are 50 percent more likely to have a stroke than White people.[1] Black men are 70 percent more likely to die of a stroke. African Americans are nearly twice as likely to have type-two diabetes than non-Hispanic Whites.[2]

If someone doesn't know by now that how we take care of our bodies will affect our overall health, they haven't been listening. If they don't know how devastating the absence of fathers is, they have had their eyes closed. It's not more information that we need—we already have plenty of that.

You don't have to be Black to be overwhelmed by the hopelessness of generational defeatism. If you travel the country just a bit, you'll see the same defeated, slouched-shouldered look among poor White people in Appalachia. You can drive just a few short miles from Sunnyside and

---

1   "Stroke and Black/African Americans," minorityhealth.hhs.gov, February 13, 2025, https://minorityhealth.hhs.gov/stroke-and-blackafrican-americans#footnote1.

2   Tianna Hicklin, "Factors Contributing to Higher Incidence of Diabetes for Black Americans," National Institutes of Health, January 9, 2018, https://www.nih.gov/news-events/nih-research-matters/factors-contributing-higher-incidence-diabetes-black-americans#:~:text=You're%20more%20likely%20to,over%20the%20last%2030%20years.

see the same look and find the same defeated attitudes in the Hispanic neighborhoods of Houston. And you will also see the same behaviors leading to similar health risks, such as stroke and heart disease.

If you were raised in isolation on a mountain somewhere and were suddenly thrust into one of these centers of despair, you might assume that people were trying to kill themselves. But I think some folks who have seen their dreams die on the vine are just trying to numb the pain until they die. They're just getting by until the end comes.

Just getting by! Just flying on autopilot! No direction! No plan! No hope!

Let's be honest here—*something has to change.* I think that anyone with a heart for other people can agree with that. But that's an easy thing to say. What is difficult for me to accept is the reality that change must begin with me.

Here's where people like me come in, people who have escaped the cycle of despair. We aren't better than the people who are destroying their lives—we've simply made different choices. Actually, we haven't made "choices"—it's really only one choice. And that choice is that we have decided to listen to a different story told by a different narrator than the one based on the lie that we are worthless. We simply chose to listen to what God says about our value.

The masses have tried to make sense of a cruel and unjust world without him, and at the end of the day, they must realize that they are still powerless and embittered! Maybe they do know this about themselves, or maybe they don't. But hopefully, at some point, they will admit their anger and frustration and begin to look upward.

Not everyone is going to be able to hear what I have to say. That's OK. Maybe later it will resonate with them.

But in short, here's my message to anyone who will listen—*God must become real to you! So must his Word! You can try to find purpose*

AUTHOR'S NOTE

in football or basketball, in dealing drugs, or in music, but it won't fulfill you. You can find your place as a doctor or a lawyer or a banker. But even if you make it to the top and make boatloads of money, you will just be a rich, angry, resentful person without a higher purpose. You'll still be just as unhappy as you were before, maybe more so because what you thought would make you happy didn't. The truth is that you won't find peace because you didn't look in the one place you can find it—you didn't pursue God.

I hope my compassion comes through in my tone because my heart is truly broken for the millions of people who live without hope. After finishing my previous book, I decided that it would be my last. But over the past few years, I've surveyed what's going on in America, and I don't like it. The only thing that has separated our country from almost all the other nations has been our commitment to the truth of God. But now, sadly, this love of truth is under attack. We are engaged in a fierce battle with those who would take it away.

But the one casualty that we cannot afford in a war like this is our relationship with Almighty God. He, and he alone, is the source of greatness because he is great himself. However, he won't share it with just anyone. Greatness is only enjoyed by people who relentlessly pursue a great God.

I don't like to stare at people, but I will sneak a glance once in a while. And when I look, what I see frightens me. I don't mean that I am afraid for myself, because I know to whom I belong. God has blessed me with an enduring identity—it can't be stolen or hijacked.

It's the kids on dates, both on their devices and completely ignoring one another. It's the young mother and father sitting at a restaurant, both glued to their phones and ignoring the kids. And it's the parents putting devices in their kids' hands to make them more manageable.

And I mourn this loss of intimacy and togetherness. The impersonal cyberworld has replaced face-to-face interaction between human beings who were created in the image of the God who is personal with us and desires us.

My prayer is that this book will change lives—one person at a time. I know I run the risk of sounding arrogant, but I need to let you know that I didn't come up with this pathway to success on my own. Instead, it is the product of decades of input I have received from an untold number of wise people who have poured into my life, beginning when I was a young boy and continuing to today. All of it, I believe, was orchestrated by God.

So, let me say this—if anyone is ready for change, then they need to be prepared for the challenge. I will promise you this: I won't beat around the bush. I will be direct and to the point. Yes, it will be challenging, but the only way to live a great life and avoid the boring and painful state of mediocrity is to work hard at doing the hard stuff.

INTRODUCTION

Sunnyside, a Community of Discouraged People

The street I grew up on in the Sunnyside community on the south side of Houston, Texas, was officially named Woodward Street, but everyone around Houston just called it the Dump Road.

It shouldn't be too hard to guess why it was called that.

The Dump Road was entirely dirt with an overlay of lime rock covered with tar, and it was periodically sprayed with used motor oil collected from the city's massive fleet of vehicles. It was sometimes muddy, sometimes dusty, but almost always deeply rutted, and it led directly to Houston's landfill, which was less than a mile from our ramshackle house in Sunnyside.

I've been away from Sunnyside for a long time now. So long, in fact, that it's hard to believe that I ever lived there. If you were to go looking for Sunnyside today, you wouldn't recognize the place I will describe to you. Developers have swept in and scooped up the land at depressed prices and built apartment complexes in place of the decaying homes. Sadly, many of the people who grew up with me can no longer afford to live there.

What I recall most about Sunnyside back in the day is that it was, in many respects, a sad place, a place where poverty ruled.

However, when I think about the people who lived there when I was a young man, they weren't all sad and hopeless people. I've classified them into three different categories. It's important for me to tell you this because I don't want to paint a picture that would create the impression that everyone in Sunnyside was broken.

The first group were the men and women who had completely surrendered their hope. There were a lot of them. They were the ones who hung out on street corners swigging on the poison that was peddled out of the liquor store. They had completely given up, thinking that, as long as the system was rigged against them, they might as well not even try.

The second group living there were the ones who, while they had not entirely given up hope, were just hanging on by a thread. They were the ones you could hear saying things like, "Ain't no sense in trying too hard. It ain't gone make no difference anyhow." But you could still find them trudging every day to their jobs, coming home, cooking supper, watching a little television, going to bed, and waking up early the next morning to repeat the same routine all over again.

They were the "just keeping their heads above water" kind of folks—good, hard-working people who had no imagination for anything better.

And then there were the occasional people who, like my mother and a few other strong Black women in our neighborhood, seemed to live above the line of despair. They found a way to comfortably dwell right there in the midst of all the junk of Sunnyside yet still emotionally and spiritually prosper in spite of it. They never caved in to the temptation to numb the pain with drink or drugs or take in a half-hearted man who would lie around, nor did they just sit around waiting for good things to come their way. They made things happen.

To this day, I thank God for those men and women because their circumstances were often just as bad as those of the rest of the community. Sometimes worse! They could have given up too, but they didn't.

When I was drafted by the Chicago Bears, I remembered a promise I had made to my mother just after my dad had bolted for greener pastures. As soon as I signed my NFL contract, I flew to Houston and proudly informed her that I was going to get her out of Sunnyside.

"Mama, it's time for me to keep my promise to you. I'm going to buy you a house in a nice neighborhood. You don't have to live here anymore."

I fully expected her to break out in tears of joy, wrap her arms around me, and thank me. But what she did next completely took me by surprise.

The way I remember it, she cocked her head to one side in one of those looks mothers are famous for and said resolutely, "What do you mean, son? Why would I want to leave Sunnyside? I've got everything I need and want right here!"

I stood there with my mouth wide open for what seemed like an eternity. I had never been caught off guard more than I was on that day. Ever since I was twelve years old, I had dreamed of rescuing my mother from Sunnyside. And I had repeated this promise to her a thousand times over the years. So, the fact that she was surprised, surprised me.

She took advantage of my pause, softened her look a little, and continued, counting her points on her fingers, "Look, son—I can walk to the dry cleaners. My church is right down the street, and all my friends are here. Why would I want to leave Sunnyside?"

In desperation, I paid a visit to my old high school coach later that day, hoping that I would find a comrade to back me up on my effort to get Mama out of the neighborhood. Coach Brown knew how tough Sunnyside was; surely, he would go to bat for me with my mom.

"Coach, I have a problem I think you can help me with. I want to move my mom to a better neighborhood and into a new house. But she doesn't want to leave."

Mama had already caught me off guard earlier in the day when she had balked at moving to a "better" community. Now, Coach was about to jerk the rug out from under me again. He crossed his arms and looked up at me from behind his desk.

"Who are you building this house for, son—you or your mom?"

I blinked in disbelief that he had even asked me such a thing. I drew a quick breath and answered with maybe more than a little irritation in my voice. "Uh, for Mama! Of course I'm building it for Mama."

"Well, if you're really building it for her, build it where she wants to live. You take her out of the neighborhood where her hairdresser, her church, and her lady friends are, and she'll be dead in no time at all."

I left his office with my tail between my legs and began to make plans to have the old homeplace bulldozed and a new one built, one just like she wanted—right in the same place on the Dump Road. It would be a modest little house with all the amenities, but it would be right there in Sunnyside, in the neighborhood where I grew up, right where Mama wanted to live.

For months, everyone rode past Mama's house, watching it rise up out of the neighborhood, and marveled, "Would you look at the house Mike is building for his mama." My mother was proud of that.

It was a statement that her confidence in God's faithfulness and all her hard work on my behalf had actually paid off.

So, yes, Sunnyside was a sad place in many ways, but there was an inner pride in that community that longed for something most people there assumed they could never have. Many of them had given up hope, but once in a while, someone like Rudell Singletary would raise up a son or daughter who managed to be successful despite the circumstances.

Mama's house became a symbol, a source of pride for everyone in Sunnyside. For a moment, people were able to think, *Well, Rudell's son made it, and look what he's done for her. Maybe there's hope for the rest of us.*

I'm glad my mother and Coach Brown won the argument. Mama joyfully and thankfully lived in that house until she left to go be with the God she had loved her entire life.

I will share in detail the process that I followed, which set me up to escape the same generational sorrow that many of my peers endured. However, before we get too far into the meat of that, let me give you a little more background information about life in Sunnyside back in the day.

LIFE ON THE DUMP ROAD

Every single garbage truck in all of Houston hurtled past our house on the Dump Road on the way to discard the putrid junk from their bellies into the rotting mountain of refuse at the end of the street. And all the way to the landfill and all the way back, the foul stench of sour milk and rotting meat whirled out of the trucks and was ferried in the wind through the entire neighborhood.

The only thing was that houses such as the Singletary house got the worst of it. We had a front-row seat because our home was standing just a few feet from the edge of the Dump Road. What I especially remember is that the dry seasons were the worst. The drivers seemed unaware or unconcerned that they were blanketing our community with white billowing clouds of dust that covered everything for fifty yards on both sides of the street.

My mother and father worked hard to feed their ten kids and put a roof over our heads. Neither of them shied away from a hard day's work, even if it meant that, at the end of the day, their clothing would be drenched in sweat and their bodies covered in dirt. But when it came to one of the frequent forays our family made out into the community for church or school events, Mama made sure that all of us were clean and dressed for success. I often heard her say, "No child of mine is going out in public looking like a tramp." When the Singletary kids went out with Mama, she made sure that we were always spick-and-span clean, sporting our Sunday best.

Her problem was that the trucks and the dust they kicked up were a threat to all the hard work she put in to make sure we were presentable to the public. So, she became a logistical expert of sorts. Once we were all bathed, dressed, and ready to go out as a family (which wasn't very often), she would stand at the door and hold us back until the dust from the latest truck settled a bit before we sprinted to the old Cadillac and packed our bodies into that old cavern of a car.

It was often a close call, but I don't remember ever getting crop-dusted by the next speeding garbage truck. We always arrived at our destination as neat and clean as we were when we left.

I was an unhealthy child from the moment I came into this world. As a matter of fact, because I was my mother's tenth child and because they spotted something suspicious in her womb, they encouraged her to terminate her pregnancy.

I am thankful that my parents decided to trust God with the outcome of my life, but I still spent more time in the hospital during the first years of my life than I care to think about. I don't know if I can put the blame on the unhealthy conditions of Sunnyside, but I do know that cancer and asthma, and other respiratory diseases, seemed to be more common in our community. Maybe it was the dust. Who knows what nasty pathogens and allergens were in those billowing clouds of grit?

SUNNYSIDE'S BAD MOOD

Sunnyside was like one of those people we all know who is always on the verge of being in a bad mood. Nothing about Sunnyside told me that I or anyone else in my neighborhood mattered. With very few exceptions, this was the place where dreams went to die.

However, as bad as Sunnyside was, it wasn't the worst neighborhood in Houston. When we compared our community to those other neighborhoods, we didn't feel so hopeless. But when we traveled just ten or fifteen minutes or so past the edge of Sunnyside and drove through the communities where affluent White people lived in isolation (and all White people were affluent compared to us), we knew the truth. "They don't live the same way we do. They aren't like us!"

Everywhere I looked, almost everything was on the edge of decay. While there were some newer houses and a few homes like ours that were well maintained with well-kept yards, there were still plenty of homes sagging on their rotting foundations too.

There were other indicators that also told the story of Sunnyside. Broken-down cars with weeds and small trees sprouting up from the engine compartments; semi-feral dogs lounging on the side of the road; young women flaunting their bodies on the sidewalks; and young men with wilting shoulders, slouching on the corners and in vacant lots, whispering secrets to one another as they cast shifty glances in all directions.

Deprivation and poverty! Until I was a little older, I had no idea there was any other way to live. I didn't think about what it would be like to live in a cleaner neighborhood or to come home to a nicer dwelling—I'd never seen anything but Sunnyside.

If Sunnyside could have talked, I think she would have offered up her resignation. "This is as good as it gets. We get the leftovers in society. It's just the way life is for people like us. Accept your lot in life. Just stay in your place and we'll all be fine, and we will all die here together."

And for the first few years of my life, there I was, bobbing along with everyone else in the same dirty stream. Everything was out of my control. I suppose that I thought deep down in my heart that this was my destiny, but to be honest, I didn't really think about it much. Everyone I knew just did what they had to do to survive.

If someone had asked me my views on the American dream, I would have simply shrugged my shoulders and replied, "What's that?" All dreams were easier said than done for young boys like me. Just like the line from the old Stevie Wonder song says, "Living just enough, just enough for the city." That was us.

I'm shocked by it now, after being away from Sunnyside for so many years, but we certainly lived up to our expectations. The only problem was that we didn't expect much. Our community could have thrown a little fresh paint on our houses and kept our yards clean. But with few exceptions, we did not. Why would we? What difference would that have made? We expected less, and we received what we expected.

THE FIRST GLIMMER OF HOPE

However, in the quiet of the night, there was a still voice in my mind that softly posed a question to me: *Is this all there is to life? There has to be more to life than this, right?*

It wasn't really a hope. It was just a question. There was nothing in my life that would tell me that I could expect more than the rest of the sad throng of Sunnyside.

But, one day, something happened that planted a tiny seed for something better. My dad, who was a hard and demanding man, ordered me to load up in that old pickup of his and travel with him across town to help him with one of his construction jobs. I don't remember now how old I was, but I couldn't have been more than eight or nine years old.

Until then, I had been too sickly to work with my father, but I was now finally healthy enough to help my dad in the family business. I don't recall many details about that day, but I do remember that, as Sunnyside began to disappear behind us, a new possibility opened up for me as we drove through the White neighborhoods of Sharpstown, Westbury, and Bellaire.

I didn't say a word to my father about it, but I thought to myself, *People actually live in neighborhoods with paved streets? And these trees lining the road—it's like driving through a tunnel.*

I silently took note of the beautiful homes nestled behind well-manicured lawns. Everything was different. No cars with flattened tires rusting in the driveways. No slouching, hopeless young men huddled together. No young ladies in skintight pants with low-cut blouses standing on the side of the road. No young men riding around with bicycles.

It was clean! It was safe! It was hopeful! At least it was if you were White. If you were Black, not so much. It may have seemed normal to

VISUALIZE YOUR GREATNESS

the folks who lived there, but to me, it was dreamy, almost surreal. I had never seen anything like it. I had no idea that other people lived that way, except for what I had seen on television. But when you see it for yourself in person, it becomes real to you—even if it seems impossible in the moment.

But I did make a mental note that day.

It wasn't a plan or a strategy yet! I had no idea how I would accomplish it, but I silently whispered to myself, "Why can't I live like this? Why can't Sunnyside look like this?" And I made a promise to myself that day: "I will live in a neighborhood like this one day! In fact, I'm going to build neighborhoods like this one day!"

As I said, nothing in my experience told me that I could ever hope for such a thing. There were a few people in Sunnyside who encouraged kids like me to *"Live out your dream! You can do it!"*

But most people ridiculed our dreams, in part because they had very few examples of folks who had actually seen their dreams come to fruition. But another reason there wasn't much encouragement was that to see someone "make it" out of Sunnyside exposed the lazy lie that it was impossible.

Unfortunately, as soon as we headed home that day, and my father turned onto the Dump Road and pulled into our yard, that tiny glimmer of hope receded into the back of my mind, where it remained dormant for a few years. Any hope that it would germinate was almost squashed by the voice of my community. I could hear nothing else—"This is your destiny, boy! Who do you think you are to expect anything else?"

SUNNYSIDE PERKS

Life in Sunnyside was tough, no doubt about it. One of the perks of living on the Dump Road, however, was that my brothers and I learned the difference between the various trucks delivering refuse to the landfill. There were, of course, the standard run-of-the-mill garbage trucks I've told you about, but there was one special truck we always kept our eyes open for. It was the dump truck from Mrs. Baird's bread bakery.

Back in the day, the bread company would dispose of out-of-date loaves by dumping them in the landfill. Sometimes, when my dad was in between construction jobs and we were short on cash, my older brothers would wait patiently behind the bushes that lined the Dump Road for Mrs. Baird's trucks to make their way to the dump. As soon as they barreled past the Singletary house, my brothers weren't far behind, their legs pumping their bicycle pedals as fast as they could go through the billowing dusty clouds. They usually arrived at the landfill just as Mrs. Baird's trucks were pulling away, and they would retrieve a few loaves of bread from the top of the heap to bring home for Mama to make sandwiches and toast.

At other times, we drove Dad's pickup to the landfill and scoured through the piles of trash and garbage, looking for old appliances and electronics. Once we unloaded them in the backyard of our house, we stripped the wiring from the guts of the televisions, washing machines, and other appliances we had scavenged, and then we burned the insulation off and sold the copper and aluminum to a junkyard down the street.

And then there was Gladys and Addie Mae's Diner, which stood directly across from our house on the Dump Road. Almost everyone from Sunnyside ate there at one time or another. Those ladies sure knew how to put a meal together—fried pork chops, greens, and pies.

But Saturday was chili day at the diner. That's when everyone came out of hiding for some of the best Texas chili I've ever eaten. The only problem was that it was also the night that men would stand around in the parking lot and yard of the diner, drinking alcohol. Unfortunately, the more they drank, the more they wanted to put their own version of Sunnyside manhood on display.

Every now and then on Saturday nights, a fleet of police cars would slide up to Gladys and Addie Mae's to break up the fights before a knife was pulled out of a hidden sheath and someone got sliced open.

During the weekdays, the diner was often frequented by the soda pop drivers. They sometimes parked their trucks in front of our home, and my brothers and I would sneak into the back of the trucks, take a few cases of soda pop to drink, and then sell the bottles for a little cash.

My Father's Legacy

I said that my father was a hard and demanding man, and that was true. He seemed cruel to me then. He was also emotionally detached. Not once did I hear him say to any one of my nine siblings or to my mother or to me, "I love you!" I guess a lot of fathers back then didn't say it much. It's one thing not to say it, but it's another to have your actions say that you don't like your family.

His cruelty was far more tangible than that, however. I don't want to get too graphic, but he often lashed out in violent fits of rage toward my mother and siblings. The physical abuse that took place behind closed doors would curdle the blood of most folks.

I could go into graphic detail about the things my father did, but you'll just have to use your imagination about that—it's just too embarrassing to talk about openly. All I can tell you is that what he

INTRODUCTION

did left a trail of incredible pain and trauma that reverberated across generations and even throughout the community.

I only mention this because, after talking to so many folks through the years about the direction of their lives, I have discovered that there are perhaps millions of people who have experienced the same kind of family trauma. It often takes place behind closed doors, where it is kept hidden for years in some secret compartment in our hearts and minds.

The problem is that when we don't heal from this trauma, these things become like little demons dwelling rent-free inside our heads. They twist reality and cloud our view of God. For the rest of our lives, we filter every relationship, every experience, and even every opportunity through them like a giant membrane that keeps anything good from passing through.

My father was a perfect example of this, of what unhealed trauma is like when it is left to fester. He didn't know that he was doing this, but he carried the baggage of his own childhood trauma straight from his father's house and put it on the backs of his own wife and children. He never dealt with it! He didn't learn a thing!

Yet, every Sunday, he would stand in the pulpit of our little Pentecostal church and preach his version of the Gospel, banging the podium and shouting at the top of his voice.

He loved the adoration and praise of the members of his congregation, most of whom had no idea what went on once our family shut the doors of the Singletary house on the Dump Road. I didn't see the irony then, but despite his own rampant unchecked sin and generational brokenness, he became an expert at passing out generous doses of condemnation on others.

It was just like he was two distinct men. On Sunday and out in the community, one of those men was the pastor, respected and even idolized. But behind the closed doors of our house, there wasn't a lot of Gospel. There, he became another man, a monster who seemed to take pleasure in tormenting those he was expected to love the most. He was overbearing, angry, and frustrated with his inability to control his family.

It was years before I realized how important fathers are in setting the tone in a home. Fathers always lead—either for good or for evil. And my father certainly led our family. But his leadership did not produce good fruit. Instead of peace, harmony, and love, our leader set a tone that manifested itself in screaming, cursing, fighting, abuse, and worse.

As the youngest child, it was easy for me to slide away from the fray and find a hiding place. I wanted no part of the drama, even when I was a little kid. Many nights, when the fighting began, I would retreat to my bed and cover my ears in a vain attempt to shut out the chaos. They usually didn't even miss me. But no matter what I did, the shrieking voice of family chaos reverberated in my ears. I will tell you later how I finally managed to distance myself from it all.

WHY AM I TELLING THIS STORY?

As I said in the foreword, I don't like telling my story. It's not that I am ashamed of it, because almost the entire story—the good and the bad—was out of my control. But it is painful to remember. Those were definitely some hard times.

However, I'm looking at the bigger picture here. This isn't about me, Mike Singletary, the Hall of Fame football player. Some people may rise to prominence and sign big contracts for no other reason than that's just how it turned out. But, in my case, I am firmly convinced that God has gifted me with the desires of my heart so that I could use both my blessings and the trauma I've endured as a platform to

INTRODUCTION

speak to people who see no way out of their own physical, emotional, and spiritual poverty.

I have lost track of the number of folks with whom I've had this conversation about a different future, a future of hope. They are people from all walks of life. And, in one sense, I had one thing in common with all of them. At one time, I too had grown tired of seeing my dreams quashed—tired of getting my hopes up only to have them dashed over and over.

They all thought they wanted to hear what I had to say. After all, most of them had sought me out in one way or another. But, sadly, the majority of them heard me, shook their heads, slumped their shoulders, and walked away. What I told them about success seemed too hard or even impossible. It was like I was speaking another language, one too foreign for them to grasp. So, they returned to the life strategies they were most familiar with; they went back to just getting by, settling for mediocrity, or caving in completely.

Think about it! Most of them were eager to talk about it, but the majority weren't ready to do anything beyond complaining about life. But success takes far more than complaining. It boils down to whether a person is willing to do the work, to formulate a plan, to create a vision for their life, and then to follow it.

The ones who walked away were unwilling to commit to the hard labor it takes to be successful. I'm convinced that all of them lacked what I had been given—they were unaware that the faint dream inside of them had been planted there by God. And since they didn't know God's purpose for their lives, they just thought it was some pipe dream, a fantasy that would never be realized in their lives.

The saddest part of not knowing the source of our dreams is that it leaves us vulnerable to the ridicule of the same kinds of people who poked fun at my vision. It's when we are unaware that our dreams for

VISUALIZE YOUR GREATNESS

something greater come from God that the words of the discouraging and ridiculing crowd do their damage.

"You're not beautiful enough!"

"You're not wonderful enough!"

"You're not smart enough!"

"You're not tall enough!"

"You're too black, or you're too light!"

And perhaps the most devastating words a person can hear: "You're too late!"

In the vacuum of not knowing God and his plan for our lives, our dreams begin to be buried beneath the accumulating muck of hurt, pain, rejection, fear, and shame.

If that is you, I want to assure you of one thing—*You are not unique! We've all been there! We all have our scars! Every single one of us! But we must find a way to turn all of those disappointments and all of those setbacks into something positive. We must find a way to move forward, a way to finish strong! If we don't, we will always be blaming someone or something for our failure. We will find any excuse we can to quit and just ride it out to the end!*

In this book, I will give you what was given to me: a seven-step formula called the "Seven *C*s of Success" that I believe will be your blueprint for real life changes. But before we begin, I would like you to get out your pen, a piece of paper, and begin to write down what it is you want out of life. Just write it down. What could that hurt?

Let's do this! Together!

PRINCIPLE 1

COURAGE

---

cour·age

/ˈkərij/

noun

the ability to do something that frightens one

---

1. COURAGE TO DREAM

I suppose I would have followed the family tradition and carried on living out my father's legacy if not for something that happened when I was about ten years old.

One day, I received a package in the mail that contained an audio version of Norman Vincent Peale's book *The Power of Positive Thinking*. This was before Audible or streaming. It was even before CDs were a thing. The entire book was on cassette tapes. That should tell you all you need to know about how long ago it was.

I still have no idea where they came from. I certainly didn't have the money to purchase them myself. I used to imagine that they were sent by an angel or something. All I know is that receiving them radically altered the trajectory of my life.

Night after night, I would retreat to my bed as soon as the fighting began, put on my little dime-store headphones, and listen to this man tell me that I could change the direction of my life by changing my thoughts and practices. He taught me to dream of a better life, one without chaos and drama. I began to imagine living in a brand-new house burrowed behind giant trees and a well-manicured lawn. I envisioned a loving relationship with my future wife. I visualized myself holding my future children in my lap and kissing them and playing with them.

My family would know that Daddy loved them because he would tell them and because he would provide for them. He would find a safe place for them to live in a community of hope. He would lead them to paint a future vision of success for themselves. It would be safe to dream in his family.

Soon after I began listening to the tapes, I recalled the day when I had gone to work with my father years before, the day when I had seen the possibility of a different life for the first time, and I began to ask myself again, *Why not me? Why not us?*

Of course, I didn't know Norman Vincent Peale when I was just a boy. I have long wished that I could have met him and told him how his encouraging words altered the course of my life. Not long after I retired from the NFL, I decided to give him a call. I was saddened when his wife said, "Mike, you just missed him. He went to be with Jesus only a week ago."

I don't know anything about his theology or the details of his life. What I do know is that, decades ago, an older White man told a young Black boy, who thought that he had no hope for a better life, that God had given him permission to dream. And that permission to dream was more enduring, more ironclad, and more irrevocable than any of the lies told to him or told in Sunnyside about his potential.

His words made all the difference in the world to me.

A couple of years after I began listening to Norman Vincent Peale, my father came home one day and asked my mom to step outside. As I said, one of the perks of being the youngest of ten kids is that it is easy to get lost in the crowd. No one pays any attention to the baby, right? So, when Mama stepped outside, there I was, right behind her. She and my father never even noticed me.

But I noticed them, and I heard what my dad said. And what he said destroyed my world.

"I'm tired of fighting, Rudell. I want out! I want a divorce!"

Everyone outside of the Singletary house thought that my father was a cut above most of the other men in Sunnyside. Kids loved him. His church members adored him.

However, no one in our house saw him that way. As a result, none of us thought our parents' marriage was healthy. We had all seen behind the mask that Charles Singletary put on as soon as he stepped outside. We knew what he was really like.

But his one redeeming quality was that he had labored hard to provide for his family, and he was the only reason we had the little that we did have. So, my mom asked the question that was on my mind too. "What are we supposed to do? How am I supposed to feed all these kids?"

My father's reply was cold, heartless, and unfeeling. "You'll figure it out." And with that, he turned and walked out the door.

There's only one thing worse than having an overbearing and abusive father, and that's having a father who is a deserter. When he walked away, I felt the gut punch that told me things were about to get a whole lot worse.

Only two months after divorcing my mom, my dad was married to a woman half my mom's age. And it wasn't long after that before they had a child together. He built her the house my mother had always asked him for until she had grown weary of asking and had just given up. And while my dad had enough money to lavish his new woman with some of the finer things Mama had never had, getting him to support us was like pulling teeth.

Within a couple of years, his new wife had kicked him out and divorced him, and by the time I was drafted by the Chicago Bears, my dad was flat broke. I had to help him move an old house onto a lot next door to my mom's house, just to put a roof over his head.

As I said, my father had never been a nurturing man. There was no encouragement from him to any of us, especially my older siblings. Almost every word that came out of his mouth was harsh and demeaning.

More than once, I witnessed my father grow frustrated with the harshness of his own life and lash out at my older brothers. "I'll die and go to hell before I see any of my boys get what I've got."

Deep down, I think I knew that he cared. But words like that are so hard that it's impossible to see the love beneath them. As a result, I don't think any of my siblings ever knew that our father actually did love them. In fact, I'm sure they didn't. Some of them carried that thought to their graves. His harsh words were often like a hot knife that left painful, festering wounds that never went away.

After I had reached adulthood and had enjoyed some measure of success, I sat down with my father and listened to him. It was then that I realized he hadn't cast a vision for our lives because he hadn't known how to do that for himself. He had always said he was destined for greatness, but I don't think he ever thought that he had a real shot at it. My dad had a dream, something he thought about, I'm sure, but not enough to make him take action.

PRINCIPLE 1: COURAGE

On the surface, he had always seemed so confident. It was only when I became a man and talked to him, man-to-man, that I realized that his confidence was nothing more than a mask to cover his insecurity and disappointment with life. He had been a beaten-down man whose hopes of a better life had been out of the reach of his imagination for his entire life.

I still condemned what he had done, but at least I understood him enough to cast off the burden of hatred for him that I had carried for so long. It was liberating! Unfortunately, all of my brothers and sisters carried the strain of that load for the rest of their lives, and that weight broke their backs. Most of them never recovered from the culture of hate, anger, shame, and fear that my father cultivated in our family. It reared its ugly head in their lives as time went on, and the weight of unforgiveness grew heavier and heavier. In the case of my siblings, the price they paid for holding on to their resentments destroyed their health and almost every single one of their relationships.

But I didn't know all of that about my father on the day he left us. There was a part of me that was happy to see him slide out the door because I knew that I would never hear another of his demeaning insults after that.

However, the blow that my mother took that day is something I will never forget. Life had been hard for her up to that point. As I said, she had worked like a dog in partnership with my father to put food on the table and a roof over the heads of her ten children. Until then, she had been barely surviving. But through that one act of selfishness, the possibility of barely surviving suddenly walked out the door along with him.

Perhaps weaker women would have surrendered to the despair. If not for her character, maybe my mother would have shuffled a few steps to Mr. Johnson's liquor store two houses down and used the few coins she had to buy a bottle of cheap gin. Others had done it! They had believed the lie that alcohol would be the perfect medication to erase that feeling of gloom that hung over them like a storm cloud.

Mr. Johnson began to peddle his fake hope when I was barely a teenager. Before then, the kids I played with in the park after school would go to the corner market and buy cookies, pop, and chips. Sadly, after Mr. Johnson opened for business, they stopped buying the childish candies, cookies, and sodas and instead began to spend their money on beer, cigarettes, and wine.

The impact on our already wounded community was devastating.

Years later, I tried to buy that liquor store from Mr. Johnson. I think he knew I would close it down, so he refused to sell it to me, even though I was willing to pay more than it was worth!

I thank God that my mother didn't turn to the solution that Mr. Johnson was selling. What she did instead is something I will never forget. It is also something for which I will be forever thankful. She fell on her knees.

I learned a lot from watching my mom take her pain to the throne of God. Trust me, she didn't hold back. Her prayers were not at all like the polite prayers people often utter in public gatherings. As she stood before her Father, she regurgitated through the tears, mucus, and wailing all of her pent-up frustration, anger, and fear. She did not accuse God of wrongdoing, but it was clear that she didn't understand in that moment what God was doing.

It was often after midnight when she cried out the most fervently. Sometimes, I would awaken and go to her bedroom to pray and weep right along with her. With all of my heart, I longed to console her. But what did I know about life? I was only twelve years old. I just uttered the only thing I knew to say: "Mama, stop crying! One day I'm going to buy you a house and take care of you for the rest of your life!"

PRINCIPLE 1: COURAGE

Despite the pain of Dad bolting for his counterfeit version of the good life, it wasn't long before my mother rose up from her fear and grief and marshaled all the resources she could. I guess she finally figured out that there was no use crying over spilled milk. After all, she had Charles Singletary's kids to provide for.

My twenty-one-year-old brother Grady volunteered to work and help support the family. Mama took on extra work. She learned to stretch a dollar further than it was intended to go. For a time, it looked like we were going to make it.

Then, on June 22, 1972, my mother received a call from a doctor at Ben Taub Hospital. "Mrs. Singletary, I'm sorry to inform you that your son Grady was involved in a horrible traffic accident tonight."

It was a tragedy that never should have happened. A drunk driver caused a multicar pileup, killing all of the other drivers except Grady. My mother's hopes were raised, though, when the doctor told her, "We think he has a good chance of making it."

However, despite his optimism, and in spite of the prayers of my mother, Grady passed away three days later at only twenty-one years of age.

When my father abandoned his family and left my mother to fend for herself and her kids, it was hard. Unbelievably hard. But Grady's death was hard on a whole other level. I don't think that any language has the words to describe this kind of pain.

My mother had conceived and carried Grady inside her womb for nine months. And from the day he had made his grand entrance into the world, my mother had cradled him in her arms, nursed him, and mothered him into manhood.

Mama had already lost one child. My brother Dale died when I was five years old. Even though I was just a young boy, I remember it in

VISUALIZE YOUR GREATNESS

vivid detail—like a nightmare. A hard freeze was headed our way, but my father had not given my mother enough money to pay the gas bill.

So, Dale found someone to sell him some coal, took it back to the room he shared with our brother Willie, and set up a makeshift grill in their bedroom. They shut the door and fired it up.

By the time my parents found them hours later, Willie was unconscious, and Dale was dead.

Losing a child is devastating for all parents. But I think the pain for mothers is far greater. I know that it was for my mom. And a lesser woman would have crumbled under the grief of Grady's death. But it wasn't just losing Grady. Getting the news that he was gone was piled on top of her other accumulating grief—Dale's death, my father deserting her and her children, working hard day in and day out just to feed her kids. And now Grady was gone too, her son and her last hope.

So, when I say that Grady's death was gut-wrenching for my mom, what I mean is that her heart was almost ripped from her chest. She would rather have had her own life taken from her or have lost one of her own limbs than have lost her son.

I had a front-row seat to all of this unbearable trauma and pain. Until then, I had believed Norman Vincent Peale. After all of this happened, however, I began to doubt God. A seed of disbelief was planted in my young mind that things were not going to get better. I whispered to myself, "Maybe all of this positive thinking stuff is garbage!"

So, as I processed it all—my father's departure, my brothers' deaths, and our generational poverty—I concluded that I could not spend the rest of my life scratching and kicking my way through to the bitter end only to wind up in the same place that everyone else in my life found themselves. Yes, I had wanted more for myself! Yes, I had wanted more for my family! And I had wanted more for my neighborhood. But this was all just too much.

PRINCIPLE 1: COURAGE

So, I prayed, "God, you gotta know that none of this makes sense—it seems so unfair."

At that point in my life, I had responded to the trauma by deciding that I would just choose to be mediocre. I made the decision that I would not go as far down the road of hopelessness as others in my community had, but I also would not set my hopes too high, because I was so weary of the disappointment of unmet expectations.

I suppose I was hoping God would rubber-stamp my lowered expectations.

However, I don't think that God was happy with my decision to settle for less, because in short order, my mother stepped in to speak the truth of God to me. She had taken notice of the sudden change of direction in my life, and she called me aside. The words she spoke to me were another turning point.

She took my face in her hands, looked me straight in the eyes, and said, "Son, I want to talk to you about this thing called 'life'. I am well aware of the fact that it seems unfair and hard to understand at this time, but when you get punched in the gut, here's what you gotta do—you dust yourself off, get back in the ring, and keep on swinging until you are the only one left. You need to understand that greatness is in you, but you can't give up!"

As powerful as those words were to me, what she said next really rekindled the fire of my earlier desires. With tear-filled eyes staring into mine, she asked me one question—"Can you be the man of the house? I ask you that because greatness is in you, son. But you will never see it if you give up now!"

I took my mother's hands in mine and assured her, "I can do that!"

2. COURAGE TO WRITE IT OUT

This is the precise moment when all those desires, those imaginings, those hopes all merged into a reality that was both future and present at the same time. I assured my mom that I could be what she asked me to be.

It was also the moment when I began to tell myself, *I can do this! I can take all of this, all my pain and disappointment, and allow God to create something that cannot be contained.* I promised my mom, myself, and God, "Come hell or high water, I can do this."

While I had spent countless hours playing tackle football with the other neighborhood boys on the grass and touch football in the streets, I had never played a single down of organized football in my life. I wasn't on anyone's team, or even on any coach's radar, for that matter. I was a skinny little kid with no real skills, other than streetball skills.

I immediately began to imagine that I was all of that. But I was more than that too. In my mind, I had already signed a college scholarship and been drafted into the NFL. My imagination was so real that I was already an All-Pro football player who had won the Super Bowl and had been inducted into the Hall of Fame.

I could close my eyes and see my mother preparing meals for the family in the modern kitchen of her new house on a tree-lined street in a quiet and clean neighborhood. She was ordering the choicest cuts of meat and finest breads and pastries from the best bakeries in town. And she was doing all of this without giving a single thought to the price of anything.

And now, for the first time, this dream was not just outside of me; it was becoming a vision inside of me, a part of me. In fact, it was so real that I didn't even need to listen to the tapes any longer. I could close my eyes and see it.

PRINCIPLE 1: COURAGE

I didn't stop with just imagining, though. In what was the most courageous act of my young life up to that point, I slid a sheet of clean paper from one of my school binders, and I wrote my vision down.

And what I wrote was very specific and very detailed. Then I pinned it to the wall of my bedroom so that I could see it and reaffirm it every day. It was a contract that I made between myself and God on behalf of my mother and my community. It was a contract with no escape clause. I was so desperate that I sold out. I boarded up all exits. I trapped myself inside my vision.

This vision was not an end unto itself, however. It's true that I wanted a better life for myself. But more than that, I was tired of seeing my mother scratch and claw just to barely get by. If she had been a mediocre woman, that would have been one thing. But Mama was anything but mediocre—she was the most driven person I had ever known, willing to do whatever she needed to do to take care of her family.

So, there I was in my bedroom with my pen and my blank paper before me and with my mother in my heart, and I began to write. I don't know how many drafts I wrote before I came up with the finished product, but there was a pile of wadded paper on the floor beside me. However, once I was satisfied that I had written down precisely what my vision was, I stretched it before me at arm's length and whispered to myself, "This is what I commit to. There is no going back. It is a done deal."

I have often wished that I still had the original paper from all those years ago, but it disappeared somewhere along the way. It doesn't matter, though, because it was the first thing I saw in the morning when I opened my eyes and the last thing I saw before I closed them at night. And I studied it multiple times during the day.

Trust me! I not only have my vision memorized, but I can clearly remember exactly what it looked like. I don't need the original—the original is a part of me.

1. Get a scholarship to college

2. Get my degree

3. Become an all-American

4. Get drafted and go to the NFL

5. Buy my mom a house and take care of her

6. Become an All-Pro

7. Go to the Super Bowl

8. Own my own business

I understand two things about my list. One, it wouldn't win me a Pulitzer Prize in journalism. And two, no banker would loan me money based solely on my vision.

But you know what? I didn't care. I was just a twelve-year-old boy. I didn't even know what a Pulitzer Prize was. And I surely wasn't thinking I would finance my dream with a bank loan. As I said, this was a three-way contract with God, my mom, and me! That's all it was, but it was more binding than anything else I had ever known. Once I had put it down on paper, I thought to myself, *Ain't no backin' out now!* Even I knew that a real man doesn't break a covenant vow.

3. COURAGE TO WAIT ... BUT NOT TOO LATE

I said that it was a courageous act on my part, and it was. It wasn't easy to hear the naysayers ridicule me with their taunts.

"Hey, guys, Mikey thinks he's going to play in the NFL one day."

"Oh yeah? He's too small, too slow, and too soft. He's gonna get knocked out."

"Little Mikey—too tiny for even the seventh-grade team!"

They were right, of course. I was skinny and undeveloped. And I'm not going to lie—the raucous laughter that followed their taunts pricked my heart. It was a little intimidating at first.

I don't know how to explain my commitment to my vision in the face of this opposition other than to say that I relied on God the whole time. I guess his voice was just louder than theirs.

Something else gave me the strength to value my vision more than I did the opinions of others. Even at that age, I knew that my vision was a slap in the face for them. Not that I'd had any intention of insulting them when I had made my contract with God, but by taking inventory of my life, recognizing the spiritual and moral poverty of my community, and then committing to excellence in my life, they felt I was calling them liars.

Their version of reality was that a man could not rise above the system that kept him down. And there I was, that skinny little boy who had never played a down of organized football, telling them that God had given him permission to dream about the NFL. Without ever standing behind the pulpit, I was preaching a sermon to everyone in Sunnyside that could have been titled, "I am a child of God! I bear his image! I matter to him, and I matter to my community. I hear his calling, and I will be faithful to it."

I knew that my vision was insulting to them, but I just chose to trust God and what I had heard Norman Vincent Peale tell me on those tapes.

But as I stood at the crossroads where my dream intersected with the words of the naysayers who tried to poke holes in my vision, I realized I had to make a decision. Yes, I had a vision, but my vision was only for the future. And I was the only one who believed it would come to pass.

All I knew at that point was that I would have to fully commit myself to preparing for my vision to be realized. I would have to wait for it as I made myself ready to enjoy it. Even then, I knew that whatever I wanted to accomplish in the future had to be greater than anything in the past. So, I burned my ship. There was now no turning back.

4. COURAGE TO FIGHT FOR WHAT GOD PUT IN YOU

In a way, my fear of ridicule was a sort of idol because I was tempted to put more stock in the opinions of my peers and the older kids who lived aimless lives than I did in my commitment to honor God.

Thankfully, the voice of my mother kept playing on a loop in my head. It overshadowed my fear and doubt and allowed me to hear the truth of God—"Mike, there is greatness in you, but you will never realize it if you give up now." I kept hearing her voice, telling me of God's love for me and that his hand was upon me.

As difficult as it was sometimes, I simply tried to courageously obey his call.

Once I was obedient in this one area, it wasn't long before I began to notice myself displaying courage in other ways. I had already practiced courage by dreaming and writing out my vision. But I soon discovered that my simple act of obedience began to bear other fruit.

I don't like to think of myself as an idol worshipper, but when I look back on the things I held dear to me at the time, I don't know what else to call myself.

For example, until the day that I stepped out in faith and wrote out the vision I had been given for my life, I didn't know anything about delayed gratification. If sugary foods were available, I ate them.

If I had the choice between exercising and sitting on the couch, I would always choose to rest.

But once I committed myself to my vision, I simultaneously committed to denying myself what I wanted in the moment and taught myself to choose what would pay dividends later in my life. Even if it was something that had no inherent evil in it, such as having a girlfriend or buying new clothes, I waited for anything that took away from my vision. Now there was nothing vague. I had to fight for this.

This took courage because almost everyone I knew lived only in the moment. It's true that they had their dreams, but that's all they were. They were waiting, too, but not in a healthy way. They were waiting for their dreams to appear out of nowhere.

Instead of delaying gratification, they worshipped the rush of spontaneous gratification, and the pressure was on me to join them. In fact, I had been headed down the same path until my mother's intervention. As I said, by not joining them and instead working to see my dream come to fruition, I was calling them liars.

There were other idols that were torn down by my courage too. By God's power, I threw the idol of timidity into the fire and learned to fight for what God had put on my heart. I learned to reject the idol of resentment as I found the power to let go and forgive.

All of this took courage. But the greatest blessing that resulted from my turning away from the things I once worshipped is that I learned to love again. I had always loved my mother and siblings. But now I was set free to love people who, on the outside, appeared to be unlovable.

5. COURAGE TO LET IT GO

If anyone is wondering how I could pull something like this off, I will point once again to my mother, who reminded me that God did not create me to center my thoughts on negativity and hatred. He, in fact, called me to center my mind on him and his love for me and all of mankind. My mother didn't even have to pull her well-worn Bible off the shelf—she knew it from memory.

> *Finally, brothers and sisters, whatever is true, whatever is noble, whatever is right, whatever is pure, whatever is lovely, whatever is admirable—if anything is excellent or praiseworthy—think about such things. Whatever you have learned or received or heard from me or seen in me— put it into practice. And the God of peace will be with you. (Phil. 4:8–9)*

I said earlier that I worshipped idols, and that was true. An idol isn't always made of gold or wood. It can be anything that controls our thoughts, other than the infinite God who has poured his love out on us. And this is the path I was beginning to travel.

When my mother quoted the verses above, I began to believe God's promise that I could think about him and dream of an intimate relationship with him. I also realized that I would never find peace of mind outside of him.

Once you have a clear vision, the meaningless glitter of life is exposed for what it is. This is when you are able to reject the path that most people are on. You see it, but you choose to get in the short line that no one else wants to be in. It's then that you can say no and fight for your vision.

6. COURAGE TO FORGIVE

It wasn't long before the truth of God began to dominate my thoughts. Instead of my old masters of resentment, fear, and unforgiveness, I noticed that noble, right, pure, lovely, excellent, and praiseworthy thoughts began to take me captive. And while many people may think slavery of any kind is evil, when a man is under the control of an infinite, all-loving God, it's a good thing because he always has my best interests at heart.

This was another decision I had to make—to let go, to break free of the control my old master had over me, and to embrace the new master who loved me relentlessly.

It was a very simple act of faith that transformed not only the direction of my life but also my identity—who I was. When I finally began to believe that I could think about myself as a man who relentlessly and passionately pursued truth, nobility, righteousness, excellence, and admirable and praiseworthy things, it set me up for a life that was far greater than the life I would have lived otherwise.

I was able to forgive even the man who had wounded me the most—my father—because of how God was rooting himself in my heart through my thoughts of him. The more I thought about God, the more easily I let go of my resentments and anger.

7. COURAGE TO LOVE

When we listen to human philosophies about what love is, they always lead us to become the opposite of God's design. Instead, the world's love is self-loving and self-absorbed. Sooner or later, this kind of *love* always winds up being about ourselves—what we can get for ourselves. This culture's definition of love asks questions such as, *How does the other person make me feel about myself? How is the other person meeting my needs? Do they complete me? Are they my soulmate?*

Perhaps this is why relationships are so disposable now. When we stop getting what we want from them, it's easy to throw them in the trash and move on to other people who can give us what we desire.

VISUALIZE YOUR GREATNESS

We'll explore more about what real love is in principle 7, but I also wanted to discuss it here because going against the grain of culture about what love really is takes courage. Too many people just can't figure out why anyone would push through obstacles in marriages and friendships in order to find true intimacy on the other side.

But God calls us to go even beyond that. Jesus commanded us to love our enemies and pray for those who torment us. This kind of love seems so radical to us because it is the exact opposite of the world's definition of love. And because it goes against the grain of the world's definition, it takes courage to stand out from the crowd in this way.

So, once God began to teach me how to truly love others, I was swimming against the tide of culture. I never accused any of my peers of not knowing what true love was. But let's be honest—the more God taught me how to love, the more it offended them. In fact, this kind of sacrificial love is offensive to the entire world. Only the person who has been transformed by God can love this way.

People who don't know God just can't understand how someone could love people who have wronged them, gossiped about them, stolen from them, or abused them in some way. I get it! It is so foreign to our natural tendencies that it just seems wrong somehow.

So yes, I completely understand why folks are so fearful of trusting God that this kind of love is transformational. But at some point (and I don't remember when), I figured something out: *If Jesus is who he claims to be, I don't have to understand how it will work out. I simply need to trust him that he's telling the truth. All I need to do is to obey him.*

It was then that I realized God did not give me a spirit of fear or timidity, but he empowered me to live in love, power, and self-discipline (2 Tim. 1:7).

I also learned that the courage to love was not the absence of fear but being empowered by the Spirit of God to be obedient to him in

PRINCIPLE 1: COURAGE

the presence of fear. In a sense, my love for God and my faith that he had me by my hand overpowered my fear. Yes, I am still afraid sometimes, but when I choose to listen to the Spirit, who constantly reminds me, "Do not fear, for I am with you," I am able to courageously press on.

At the end of the day, there's nothing special about me. It's not hard to be courageous when you walk with a mighty God who loves you.

PRINCIPLE 2
CONSCIOUSNESS

---

con·scious·ness

/ˈkänSHəsnəs/

noun

the state of being awake and aware of one's surroundings

---

1. CONSCIOUS OF OUR THOUGHTS

He was an enormous physical specimen. I don't remember his real name, but everyone in Sunnyside just called him "Big Bubba." There was hardly a soul in our community that didn't know who he was. And they thought they knew his character too. For all anyone knew, he was destined to be a star football player.

More than once, I overheard the older men talking about him in the barbershop and at Glady and Ina Mae's Diner. "I tell you what, if anyone's got a shot at making it to the NFL, it's Big Bubba. Have y'all seen how hard he works?"

And to be sure, Big Bubba was, for all appearances, radically committed to preparing himself to be successful on the field. When the other guys were eating greasy hamburgers, french fries, and milkshakes, Big Bubba was eating salads loaded with healthy proteins. At all hours of the day, he could be seen running and sweating through the unpaved streets of Sunnyside.

Big Bubba was not only smart, but he was influential among his peers, a very popular young man. The girls loved him, and so did his teammates and coaches.

It was a murmur that rumbled through the streets, barber shops, and cafés of our community: *Have you seen how hard Big Bubba works? That boy is gonna make it, you mark my words!* He became a metaphor, a symbol of all the dreams of the old men in Sunnyside.

The only problem for Big Bubba was that he had a fatal flaw—he just loved to hear the applause. It was true that he had everything going for him: the physical body, the commitment to intense workouts, and the recognition from his community. But it was this last part that sunk his ship—his desire for approval. As a result, he had no boundaries. Nothing to keep the bad stuff out or keep the good stuff in. If it brought him applause, he was willing to do it. If no one was cheering him on, he didn't do it.

Big Bubba did not have the heart of a champion because everything he did was for himself, for the laughs at his jokes and the cheers he received.

By the time I was a sophomore, I had already been meditating on my written vision for two or three years. Every day, and sometimes multiple times each day, I had been rehearsing it in my head. Not only that, but I had been praying fervently to God to mold me and shape me into the kind of man who would always bring glory to his name. And even more than that, I continued to plead with him to

PRINCIPLE 2: CONSCIOUSNESS

put obstacles in my way to keep me from the path of mediocrity in the most important areas of my life. I desired excellence.

It wasn't long before my coaches took note of my fervent passion in practice. And even though Big Bubba had been known as the leader, and even though he was three or four years older than I was, Coach Brown tasked me with leading the practices as team captain instead of Big Bubba.

Everyone saw Big Bubba running the streets and grunting in the weight room. But they never saw me. That's because night after night I was alone in the garage of our home on the Dump Road. In solitude, I was lifting the weights I had made by filling cans and buckets with wet concrete with a rusty iron pipe as my bar.

Not only that, I ran drills every night, over and over, perfecting my skills when my teammates were partying with Big Bubba and while the old people were in their houses watching television or listening to the radio.

I did all of this out of sight of the crowd that patted Big Bubba on the back. I wasn't out to impress them because I had not made a contract with the guys in the barber shop or the diners—my covenant was with the Almighty.

Someone might say to me, "High school is a time to have fun, to sow your wild oats. Don't you feel like you missed out?"

Well, sowing wild oats is exactly what Big Bubba did. Always the life of the party, the one with the stuff to get the party cranking. He even tried to tempt me with marijuana once in front of my teammates. He was trying to pressure me to be what he thought was a man.

"Singletary, you way too uptight! Take a hit off this baby! It'll relax you!"

When I refused to tag along behind Big Bubba and his pack of puppies, they were enraged. I don't remember understanding then why they were angry with me, but I do now. They were mad for the same reason my peers and the older boys had earlier ridiculed the vision for my life that I had posted on my bedroom wall. By not running with the pack and by living for a higher purpose, I was calling them all liars. That wasn't my intention, but it was how they saw it. In their minds, I had exposed their version of the good life as a falsehood.

What they didn't know, what very few people knew, is that I wasn't doing what I was doing hoping to get a standing ovation. As I said, when I wrote down my vision and nailed it to my wall, I was declaring that the covenant vow I had made between myself, my mom, and my God would, from that day forward, be the motivation for everything I would do. And yes, I wanted God's blessing for myself, but more importantly, I wanted it for Mama and Sunnyside. And even more importantly than that, I had come to desire God's presence in my own life more than I wanted anything else. God created a passion in me to see his face.

God had blessed me with a keen desire to bring glory to his name, and that was far more powerful than my desire to bring glory to Mike Singletary. This consciousness of God's presence hung over me like a protective shield and jealously guarded my heart.

No one ever said about me what they said about Big Bubba. They may have said it later, but not when Big Bubba was a senior and I was a scrawny sophomore. To my knowledge, not once did any of the old men in the barber shop or at Glady and Ida Mae's Diner or anywhere else in Sunnyside say about me, "If anyone's got a shot at the NFL, it's that Singletary boy." Instead, all their eyes were focused on Big Bubba. Big Bubba was a beautiful human being. Things came easy for him, including being athletic.

I sometimes mourn the wasted talent of Big Bubba. I wish he could have made it too. But I am grateful for the lesson I learned by

PRINCIPLE 2: CONSCIOUSNESS

watching him—that applause lasts only for a very short time. If I had been more conscious of the clapping hands and loud raucous cheers, I might have fallen into the same mediocre life he fell into once the cheers of high school football faded away into the dark Friday nights after the game clock wound down to zero.

But this was the difference between Big Bubba and me. In his mind, he was on his own with no thought of an infinite God who adored him. That's not to say that God didn't love him; he did—immensely. His problem, however, is that, as far as I ever knew, he wasn't conscious of it at all. But I was. For whatever reason, I was aware that God knew me, and that I could not only know him but also enjoy him.

In my case, I had burned all the bridges to my past life and my former way of thinking. I was all in, totally sold out. But in Big Bubba's case, he had an exit strategy, and it had to do with his love of approval. If he didn't make it, he could always say, "It's not my fault. You saw me working. You cheered me on! Remember? It's not my fault I didn't make it!"

We are all driven by something. And I get it—the love of the crowd can be appealing. I've been tempted by it more than once in my career. Very few people ever hear sixty thousand fans screaming deliriously after they delivered a vicious hit on the ball carrier.

It is intoxicating! No doubt about it! And it seems real! You want it to last forever! The only problem is that it doesn't last, and it isn't even real. It is the very definition of fleeting. Here today and gone before the day ends. It doesn't take long before the fans move on to someone younger who plays with more intensity.

If I were to visit the football stadium at Baylor University or Soldier Field on game day today, and even if the announcer told the crowd that I was on the fifty-yard line, waving, I might receive a lukewarm and polite smattering of applause. But even that wouldn't last long. The fans have moved on from me, but that's just part of life.

So, if we are driven by our thoughts of human approval, we will find ourselves between two unattractive outcomes. Either we will experience the haunting memories of fading accolades, or we will be forced to become more outrageous in how we live our lives. The crowds always want more. Trust me! I know!

Either way, it always comes to an end. I knew early on that I could not physically play football forever. I was conscious of the fact that a day was looming on the near horizon when I would hang up my cleats and walk away to another life. So, while I appreciated the cheers from the stands, I was actually only worried about and focused on honoring God.

Sadly, when all the approval stops is when some former players spiral out of control, as they find that what they lived for is no longer an option for them. Sometimes, even if they still desire to put on the pads, no one wants them anymore. At that point, it's over for them, and they have nothing to live for at that point.

In case you haven't picked up on it yet, I'm not just talking about sports. I'm so thankful that God's grace gifted me with a consciousness of a higher purpose than applause. Sometimes, when I am asked to speak at one event or another, the small crowd will offer a polite and restrained standing ovation. But I will never hear what I once heard in high school on Friday nights, Saturday afternoons at Baylor University, or on Sundays in Chicago.

And you know what? I'm OK with that ... more than OK, because, early on, I set a different vision for my life that led me to be conscious of the commitment I had made all those years earlier that I would pursue God. If I have his approval (and I do, by his mercy), I have all I need.

PRINCIPLE 2: CONSCIOUSNESS

The way this has played out in my life is that my consciousness of God's presence has transformed me in all other areas of my life besides football. Yes, it made me a better player. But football was only a vehicle to take me where I wanted to go. It helped me accomplish the bigger goals I had for my life and gave me a platform to tell others about the love my God has for all of us, and to help people from all walks of life be better.

But by my practice of purposefully being conscious of how I thought about playing football, I also became keenly conscious of how I lived out the more important areas of my life.

The first thing I became conscious of was the thoughts that I allowed to live in my mind. This was my first step into excellence. It would have been easy to allow the words of some of my brothers and their friends to live in my thoughts.

"Who do you think you are, boy?"

"Yeah, scholarships are for the kids from the other side of town, not for us! You didn't know that?"

"He right! That's the way it's always been for us, and ain't nothin' gonna change!"

It was hard to hear, but not because their words made me want to rip my vision from the wall and tear it to shreds. The real reason I didn't want to hear it is that I didn't want to waste my time hearing what I knew was a lie. I knew what I believed to be true, and I knew the depth of my commitment to my vision. I had no doubt about that.

As I've already said, people who have no vision and who have settled for mediocrity or less feel threatened by someone with a vision. Remember what I said? Your vision exposes the lie that things are impossible.

The raucous laughter I received was the lazy man's way out of taking responsibility for the direction of their own lives. It's the easy

43

VISUALIZE YOUR GREATNESS

way out because negatively weighing in on another man's dream, and then offering up a thousand phony reasons why it won't work, didn't require anything from them at all. Poking fun at my vision was the easiest thing any of them ever did.

Had I listened to them and allowed those thoughts to simmer in my mind, I would have stayed where I was (or worse), making almost no progress at all. I would have been just like Big Bubba, who did all the right outward things but forgot to have the same diligence toward his inner thoughts.

A few years ago, I stumbled across some medical information that explains the importance of choosing the right things to think about. In the back of all our brains is a pencil-shaped network of neurons called the reticular activating system (RAS), which is responsible for how we filter information.

You probably never think about it, but all our brains absorb millions of bits of data every day. Doors closing! A baby crying three aisles over in Walmart! A driver four cars in front of us tapping his brakes. A bird chirping! The thing is that all of this is taken in by our brains, but we take notice of only a small part of it.

If you want to put this to the test, just put this book down for a few minutes and simply sit. Don't talk! Don't multitask! Just sit and observe what's going on around you. You'll notice that the refrigerator is humming or a UPS truck is passing by just outside your living room. All of this has been going on the whole time, but you never took note of it.

The RAS doesn't distinguish between good or bad; it's just trying to give us what it thinks we want.

It works sort of like this: Let's say you take a ride in your friend's brand-new Corvette. After a while, he stops on a curvy road in the middle of nowhere, gets out, walks around to the passenger side, and tells you to switch places with him.

PRINCIPLE 2: CONSCIOUSNESS

As soon as you begin to accelerate, you realize that you've never felt such a surge of power in a car before. The machine takes the S-shaped curves like it's nothing. The smell of the Corvette's luxury leather is like nothing you've ever smelled before.

You are only a minute or two into your drive when you realize, *I'm in love with this car!*

When you get back home, you do a Google search for new Corvettes. You retrieve your financial calculator from the drawer in your desk and try to find a way to justify buying your own Corvette. The more you look, the more the desire for one begins to dominate your every thought. You visualize yourself driving across the country with your wife. You dream about the admiration you'll receive from your friends. You tell yourself, *One day, I'm going to own one of these machines.*

Then a funny thing begins to happen. Everywhere you turn, you begin to see Corvettes. They weren't there a week or two earlier, but now you can't turn the corner without seeing one. It's like a miracle or something.

The truth is, however, that nothing miraculous happened at all. Those same Corvettes were there before you began to fantasize about owning one. What really happened is that you told your RAS that you had a good emotional experience in your friend's car. And then you started feeding it more and more data. Suddenly, your eyes were opened, and you saw them everywhere you looked.

We're talking about Corvettes, but it's the same process in almost every area of our lives. For example, let's say I have a dispute with someone I was once good friends with. I start telling myself that I don't like that person anymore. It's not long before my RAS begins to provide me with evidence that I am right about that person. They make a comment that would have at one time seemed harmless or even humorous, but now it really gets on my nerves or even angers me.

45

VISUALIZE YOUR GREATNESS

And while we are at it, this explains how a couple who were once madly in love with one another can wind up hating one another so much that they end up in divorce court. It also explains our addiction to drugs, alcohol, and pornography. The RAS gives us what it thinks we want. It is our little slave, buried in our brains, and it will feed us what we feed it.

The good news is that the RAS is trainable, and the way we do that is to feed it what we really want. I have a five-step process for doing this. I'll cover each of these in isolation throughout this book, but if you want the short version, here it is:

1. Write out your vision and repeat it out loud several times each day.

2. Close your eyes and visualize yourself accomplishing your vision.

3. Go back to steps one and two immediately when old thoughts begin to emerge. Don't let those old strategies simmer in your mind. Replace your negative thoughts with your goal.

4. Take steps to accomplish your goal. Pray! Meditate!

5. Repeat steps one to four over and over and over again.

Why is this important?

I've found most people believe their lives are shaped by their life circumstances, by things that happen to them, stuff they had no control over. We think, *It's not my fault! After what happened to me, I have no control over it.* However, it's really our thoughts that determine our outcomes. I'm only responsible for the input; my RAS will do the rest.

PRINCIPLE 2: CONSCIOUSNESS

I fully understand the temptation to assume that I am shaped and molded by my circumstances. When a person is born into generational poverty, for example, the evidence seems to suggest that they are predestined to live impoverished lives too. Our observations also seem to say that people who experienced childhood sexual trauma are predestined to live caught up in a web of dysfunctional and self-destructive behaviors.

I am not saying that poverty-driven and sexual abuse traumas aren't real. They are very real, and they often serve as filters for every experience for the rest of our lives. And on a personal level, I am heartbroken every time I hear an adult recount the horror of being victimized in childhood by someone who should have protected them.

But this is what I'm talking about. For anyone who wants to be free from the negativity that has taken them prisoner, what I'm saying about the importance of choosing what we think about should be good news. There is a pathway to freedom from the demons of the past, and it's found in what we train our minds to think about.

Trust me! My own trauma, which resulted from generational poverty, racism, and the abuse from my father, was real. But if I had waited until I received justice for all the junk I experienced in my childhood before I could move on, I would still be waiting, just rehashing the same tired complaints but never experiencing real victory.

Anyone who wants a new life that is free of all that garbage needs to know that this is the starting point once they have decided to allow God to reorder their desires.

So, let's talk about that—specifically talk about which thoughts we need to bar from having access to our minds and which ones we need to nurture.

2. CONSCIOUS OF OUR POWER

"You ain't going nowhere, son. You oughta go back to truck driving."

We laugh about it now, but I'll bet it wasn't funny when Jimmy Denny, the manager of the Grand Ole Opry, said this to Elvis Presley.

I wonder if old Jimmy ever wished he could eat those words.

Elvis, by anyone's estimation, was a wildly successful musical artist, selling over six hundred million records. But success did not come easily for him. He failed his music classes in school, was somewhat of a social misfit, and was rejected by a music ensemble he had auditioned for when they told him that he just couldn't sing.

Yet, he became so well known for his music that we don't even have to say his last name for others to know whom we're talking about—just Elvis! That's it! Just Elvis!

I titled this section *power*, but someone else may call it *strength*. It's also a lot like the previous section, *Conscious of Our Thoughts*, because we will never possess the power until we change how we think.

Before we go any further, I need to make certain that you are hearing me correctly. I'm not talking about some kind of pull-your-self-up-by-your-bootstraps strategy where you grit your teeth, put your shoulder to the wheel, and force yourself to change.

Thinking like that is rooted in something far different from what I'm talking about. The bootstrap method relies on the strength and wisdom of the individual. It may serve to make a person successful in one area of their life, but it won't empower us to enjoy the total life change that I'm saying is possible. I've known many athletes who were excellent at performing on the court or the field but were failures at being a husband, father, or citizen.

What I am suggesting is the kind of change in our thinking that permeates everything. It's our power. When I heard Norman Vincent Peale and began to choose to think about good things and envision

PRINCIPLE 2: CONSCIOUSNESS

them as permanent character traits, it didn't just make me a good middle linebacker; it radically impacted how I lived in all areas of my life. I was a better student, a better son, a better brother, and a better friend.

Not only that, but this outlook continues to make me better even today. I'm a better father, grandfather, and husband than I would have been had I not chosen to think about excellent, praiseworthy, and admirable things.

In other words, I didn't find the power to succeed in life inside my own head. Not at all. I discovered it by pursuing God and listening to him. I replaced my thoughts with his Word. I didn't know that I was doing it at the time, but I trained the RAS that God embedded in the back of my brain to validate my good and right thoughts. At this point in my life, it's like muscle memory.

If you want the power to succeed, let me ask you a question that may seem silly to you at first: *Do you really want to be healed?* I ask you that because if you find yourself making excuses for why you fail, I'm not sure you're there yet. The power to change begins with being extremely uncomfortable with how we've been living, when we grow tired of the consequences of our bad decisions.

When we say things like, "Man, the system is corrupt. It's impossible for a man to get ahead," or "The White man is holding me down," or "Black people get all the breaks," we are actually saying that we are very comfortable in our failing lives.

If that's you, I want to tell you something that will shock you—all the power you need to change is right before your very eyes. Like Dorothy in *The Wizard of Oz,* who always had the power to return to Kansas, you have the power to change.

All Dorothy had to do was click her heels together. All you have to do is abandon your bad habit of complaining and begin focusing

VISUALIZE YOUR GREATNESS

on what God has already put in you. No matter where you are, or who you are, or how bad you think something is, this is the only way out if you really want to succeed.

You already have the power—just use it!

3. CONSCIOUS OF HOW WE SPEND OUR TIME

There is just something about time. You can't save it, yet it can absolutely be wasted; many people crave it, and the dying would do anything to regain it.

But you? You're here! You've still got time!

I am blessed with the opportunity to travel around the country and meet all kinds of folks. Years ago, I decided I would ask everyone I met one question: If you had it to do all over again, what would you do differently? I especially like to pose this question to people who have had some measure of worldly success, particularly those who are older than I am.

I get all kinds of responses. Some look at me sheepishly and confess that they let the love of their life slip away. Business, pleasures, and other worldly pursuits took priority over the one relationship that should have been the most important.

Others hang their heads low and look at the floor. "Mike, I messed up my son. He was such a good kid, but I just rode him until I drove him away!"

And then there are those who wish they had taken better care of their bodies so that they could enjoy their golden years. Or the men who burst into tears as they recall their unwillingness to seek help for their addictions.

PRINCIPLE 2: CONSCIOUSNESS

"Mike," one man blubbered in between sobs, "I lost everything—my family, my friends, my job ... everything. I lost it all because I just couldn't quit drinking until it was too late."

It is always amazing, however, when I ask that same question of people who have used their time wisely. They have also faced obstacles and hurdles, but rather than caving in and making excuses, they persevered and won.

The difference between these two groups of people (mostly men) is in how they have used their time. One group had wasted their time on stuff that, while it seemed urgent, really didn't matter. By the time they realized their miscalculation, it was often too late.

The other group, however, were able to identify what really mattered and had devoted their time to nurturing those things. They had the presence of mind to value time. They were keenly aware that, as I said at the beginning of this section, time cannot be saved, but it can certainly be wasted. These people are the ones who have been able to step away from the pressing business of work to recenter themselves and find balance.

I learned this lesson the hard way after I retired from football. I had made some money that gave me a significant financial cushion. So, my wife Kim and I decided that I would take a step back and not search for a job I didn't really need.

I wanted to try to make up for the lost time with her and our older kids. I'll admit that I was a little out of balance when I was playing the game, and my family suffered for it.

Not long after I retired, Kim looked me in the eye one day and said, "Mike, you're here, but you're not really here." I wanted to say, "What do you mean? I'm standing right in front of you," but I knew what she meant. I was present in body, but I was emotionally, spiritually, and mentally unavailable. To borrow a football cliche, my head was not in the game!

Thankfully, I was able to clear my mind and center my attention on what was most important to me: my wife and kids. The result of that decision was that I was shocked at how much I had missed with them.

I knew that I would never get that time back, but I committed myself to making up for the minutes, hours, and days that had been lost and to lavish more love and attention on them than I ever had before. Football had been my job, but my family became God's most precious gift to me as soon as I said, "I do!" The problem was that I had not been acting like it.

I wasn't a bad father compared to many of the dads I knew, but I figured it was time for me to redeem those lost opportunities and spend my time pouring energy and time into those who mattered more to me than any teammate, any coach, any championship, or any statistical category in which I had excelled on the field.

So, thanks to Kim, I committed myself to a keen awareness of how I demonstrated my love and passion for my family. Finally, I was there—really there. Kim never had to accuse me of not being emotionally and spiritually present for my family again.

This is a key to real success: deciding what the vital things are in your life and carving out the time to make certain that they receive the attention they deserve before it's too late.

4. CONSCIOUS OF THE COMPANY WE KEEP

"You will meet a lot of associates in this life, but your true friends will always be there." Rudell Singletary

PRINCIPLE 2: CONSCIOUSNESS

Not too long after I walked into Mrs. Lawson's fourth-grade classroom at Sunnyside Elementary School, I met one of my best friends for life.

Almost fifty years ago! Wow! When I put a number on it like that, it almost seems inconceivable to me that it's been that long. But Ron and I have been brothers in a way that transcends DNA for almost an entire lifetime.

High-profile athletes and entertainers are constantly bombarded with offers of friendship and partnerships from people who want a piece of their pie. Sadly, that is often all they want. They don't really know you as a person, and they surely don't love you.

However, they will sometimes tell you what you want to hear to get some of what you have.

"You're amazing, Mike!"

"You're the best middle linebacker ever, Mike!"

"I'm your number one fan!"

Or maybe they want to be "friends" with you only so they can tell their friends that they're buddies with a well-known celebrity. We all know the song.

I learned early on that very little of the praise was real, and almost none of it was in my best interest. Plus, I certainly didn't need anything to inflate my ego. My ego was big enough already.

What I did need were friends like Ron, who was never overly impressed with my accomplishments. Yes, he was happy for me, but it didn't change his commitment to me to hold my feet to the fire and keep me grounded in what was real. I didn't need an admirer; I needed a warrior who would fight for me and with me. Keep it real—out of love and not judgment.

Over the long years that we've been brothers, we've held one another up during the loss of our parents and siblings, trouble with

VISUALIZE YOUR GREATNESS

raising kids, and job insecurities. Through all the highs and lows, he has been a familiar voice of reason. I'm not overstating things when I say that I can't imagine going through life without Ron by my side.

I didn't know just how right Mama was about lifelong friendships when she said it, but I do now.

With no offense to Ron, the very best friend I have on this earth is my wife, Kim. Trust me, her willingness to hold me accountable is uncompromising. But more than that, she is my partner in every single area of my life. I don't make a business decision, or buy a new car, or make travel plans without running it by her first. I do that because I value her as my lover and my friend above all other relationships.

As my mother said, Kim is a true friend who will be with me forever.

But then there are the other kinds of "friends" I've had over the years. I often shudder to think about how things would have turned out for me if my mom had not confronted me about the four boys I was hanging out with in junior high school. It's sad to think about it now, but they all wound up living and behaving in ways that finally destroyed every single one of them.

When you're conscious of the company you keep, you are conscious of the impact they have on how you are molded, shaped, and formed. We need to be vigilantly aware that we are who we hang around with. We can't avoid that!

5. CONSCIOUS OF THE WORDS WE SPEAK

If you never had your father "cuss you out," you won't know what I'm talking about. I've had a lot of people say some nasty things to me in my life, but the words that my dad said to me, my mom, and my siblings left the deepest and most painful wounds.

PRINCIPLE 2: CONSCIOUSNESS

As I told you before, I didn't get off to a great start in life. For the first years of my life, I was a sickly little boy. And during those years, I followed my mama around, crying and sucking my thumb, playing the role of the baby of the family. I'm sure I milked it for all it was worth.

I clearly remember other adults telling my mother, "Looks like Mike's gonna be the runt of the family. He's not like your other boys."

Maybe adults don't realize that kids hear what is said about them in front of them, but some of the things my mother's and father's friends said about me threatened to become my identity.

What none of those people knew was that I had a secret weapon. Being the youngest kid out of ten allowed me to slip away unnoticed by the rest of our family and sit in front of the television. One actor who captured my attention was John Wayne. He was tough! He was rugged! And he always told it like it was! Despite the obstacles he faced, where it seemed like he would lose, he always won in the end.

A few years later, I fell in love with the Dallas Cowboys. One particular player I really liked was their quarterback, Roger Staubach. He was like John Wayne to me. He always knew the right thing to say, was tough as nails, and always seemed to find a way to win.

I never knew John Wayne or Roger Staubach personally at the time, so it's possible that their private lives were far different from their public personas. But what I saw in them on television kindled a spark in me that allowed me to talk to myself about who and what I wanted to be. Rather than repeating the words of my elders like a parrot that told me I was destined to be the runt of the litter, I told myself over and over again, "I am tough as nails! I will train myself to always say the right thing! I will find a way to win!"

I heard and saw those examples on television, but I also heard positive conversations between the adults in my life. I heard my dad when he talked to others. He was encouraging, understanding, and

VISUALIZE YOUR GREATNESS

caring. When he negotiated for jobs, he was firm but respectful, and he was willing to walk away from a job if he felt like it wasn't right. He always held his head up and looked them in the eye. I always admired that; he was a leader.

These words that I spoke to myself changed the direction of my life. We all go where our thoughts and words tell us to go. The good news for me is that I stopped thinking of myself as a sickly, thumb-sucking, crying little runt, and I began to tell myself that I was a man and a leader of men. And, after a while, I began to tell myself that I was chosen by God and blessed by him to lead other people out of the messes they had made for themselves and into a relationship with him.

And what do you know! I began to believe it, and it all began to come together when I was twelve years old.

But what about the young boy who doesn't have a strategy for dealing with his mother telling him that he's too lazy or too stupid? Or the young girl who only knows the words her father spoke when he told her she was too fat or too ugly or too stupid?

I'm convinced that there are millions of kids in America and around the world today whose only assessment of their worth and ability is the hateful words that the adults in their lives have spoken over them. Words that shape and mold them to see themselves as garbage.

If you've ever been in a toxic relationship with someone who held sway over you by using their words as their weapon of choice, you know what I'm talking about. Words can cut just as deeply as a razor blade. The bruising from a verbal beating doesn't leave a visible mark, but it's often deeper and lasts longer.

This is exactly what the Bible says about our use of language: "Do not let any unwholesome talk come out of your mouths, but only what is helpful for building others up according to their needs, that it may benefit those who listen." (Eph. 4:29)

PRINCIPLE 2: CONSCIOUSNESS

6. CONSCIOUS OF OUR EXAMPLES

By the time I was drafted by the Bears, the famous Walter Payton had already been on the team for a few years. Within the Bears organization, he was known as the guy with the great personality, the guy who laughed a lot and told funny jokes. He especially had a reputation for pranking his teammates.

I had heard about that, so when I got to training camp, I wanted to set the tone in our relationship. I've never been particularly fond of practical jokes, so when he came up to me, looking suspicious, kind of ornery, and like he was up to no good, I looked him straight in the eyes and said, "Walter, I don't do well with jokes and pranks, and I rarely laugh!"

It's possible that I was a little over the top, but I was there for one reason and one reason only—to complete my vision and to help the team get to the Super Bowl and win it.

A few years after my rookie season, I felt a pull in my spirit to speak to Walter about something I didn't know about. Even to this day, I don't know the specifics of what was going on in his life at that time. The message I was to deliver to Walter was simple: *Just stop it!*

My first response was, "God, I barely know him." But I knew that it would only be a matter of time before I would follow through with what I felt in my spirit I had to do.

Not long after that, we had a team event away from the training facility. Walter looked at me and said, "Hey, Mikey, you're gonna ride with me." We hadn't gone very far before Walter glanced at me with a wry smile and said, "Why you staring at me, Mikey?"

"Walter, you may wanna pull over. I have something to say to you."

He pulled into a hamburger joint, put his car in park, and said, "OK. What is it, Mikey? What's wrong?"

VISUALIZE YOUR GREATNESS

I don't know what he expected me to say, but I do know that I just came out with it. I didn't try to sugarcoat it to make the bitter medicine easier to swallow. I just said what I felt God had put in my spirit to say.

"Walter, I feel like God has given me something to tell you."

He looked at me like he had been expecting this.

"Just stop it!" I told him. "Whatever you're doing, just stop it." Then I closed my mouth and didn't say another word.

I fully expected him to fly into a rage and order me out of his car. Instead, tears formed in the corners of his eyes, and then he began to cry. I just sat there and looked ahead. I didn't know what to do, but I knew God was speaking to his heart. I had done what I needed to do! I didn't say anything more, and neither did Walter. We just drove to the event. Neither of us ever brought the subject up again. After that, we both kind of went our separate ways.

A few years later, Walter and I found ourselves living less than a mile from one another in Barrington, a forty-minute drive from our practice facility in Chicago. Walter had moved out there first and built a beautiful home. Kim and I moved there a little while after Walter and Connie because we wanted to be closer to our church.

Even though we lived so close to one another, we didn't spend a lot of time hanging out. But, one day, I was working from home when I heard the doorbell ring. I walked to the door, opened it, and standing before me was Matt Suhey, our teammate from the Bears.

Matt's eyes were sad. He looked away for a moment, as if trying to avoid eye contact, and then he said, "Walter's in your garage. He wants to talk to you."

I began to walk toward the garage with my stomach in my throat. I could tell from Matt's face that Walter wasn't just dropping by to have a cup of coffee with me. I had heard the rumors that he wasn't doing well. So, when I opened the door to the garage, I wasn't surprised to see Walter sitting on a chair with his head in his hands, tears once again filling his eyes.

"Mike, I'm sick! It's not good!"

As I said, I had heard through the grapevine that he was sick, but I'd had no idea that it was this bad. I listened as he told me the sad tale of his diagnosis and the hopeless prognosis the doctors had given him. It truly broke my heart. I loved Walter.

"Brother, I hate to hear that. What can I do for you?"

What he asked of me next confirmed the words I had felt God speak to me all those years before. It also confirmed the fact that my dedication to setting a good example had paid off. The way I see it, if I had not been so conscious about how I lived in both my public and my private life, the conversation would have never happened. By my example, which I had radically tried to protect, Walter felt that there was something different about me.

"Mike, I want you to come by my house and read the Bible to me and pray over me every day until you can't."

I'm not going to lie; I had to fight back the tears with everything in me. That wasn't only because of Walter's impending death or because of his genuine repentance that I had prayed so long for, but also because of God's faithfulness to honor my own obedience and repentance when my flaws began to rear their ugly heads.

Whatever it was that God wanted Walter to stop, I'm just thankful that God chose me to deliver the message to someone that I had a great deal of respect for. I didn't know it when I had the first conversation with Walter, but I believe God was at work.

Kim and I have often talked about how, in the moment, it sometimes seems so costly to shun the life that almost everyone else is living. I mean, who wants to stand out like a sore thumb? But when God

VISUALIZE YOUR GREATNESS

comes through and allows you to be a part of something so beautiful, it confirms our commitment to honor God by our obedience.

We don't see Connie much these days, but Kim and I have maintained our friendship with his dear wife and two children over the years. In fact, when I asked her if I could tell this story, her response was instant: "Absolutely, yes!"

All I can tell you is that whether or not you desire to set a good example boils down to your purpose for living. If you think your purpose is only to satisfy yourself, you probably won't see the importance of it. But if your inner desires are to glorify God by living an eternal kind of life right here and right now, you'll get what I'm saying. My prayer is that someone will see the example I'm setting and, instead of simply saying, "Mike Singletary is a great guy," they will be able to have some glimmer of hope that God can work in their life too. Trust me; it keeps me on my knees.

7. CONSCIOUS OF MAKING THE MOST OF EVERY DAY

Guess what I saw when I woke up this morning?

I got out of bed, washed my face, and sat down at the table in our kitchen. I looked outside, and the sun was coming up in the east.

Would you believe it! It was a new day! It was a lot like yesterday, except yesterday was gone! And by the time that you read this, today will no longer be today either. It will be in the history books as well.

And with this new day, I have new opportunities! I have new choices to make! No matter what I chose to do with yesterday, or even a thousand yesterdays, I can choose to make the most of every opportunity that presents itself to me today.

And the most important choice I have before me today is whether I will wallow in my past failures or rest on my past accomplishments,

PRINCIPLE 2: CONSCIOUSNESS

or if I will leave it all behind me and press on toward the goal that lies before me.

A lot of people live on autopilot, which is a good thing if we've been putting habits, practices, and rituals into place that will lead us to be successful. I'll talk about this in more detail later, but for years, I've been meditating on God's Word and the vision he gave me, exercising my faith, and praying every single day for God to reveal more of his plan to me. Kim and I carve out time every day just to talk, dream, and pray together. It's like clockwork to me now. I don't even have to think about it; I just do it.

However, if we are simply taking what the day gives us, and we have no rituals and practices that form and shape us into better people, we won't get very far. One sad day begins to look like all the other sad days. And once enough of those unproductive days add up, we soon feel stuck in that pattern.

Of the thousands of people I've had conversations about success with over the years, I don't recall a single person who didn't long for a better life than the one they were living. Some were hotly pursuing their dream every single day, trying to improve by consciously practicing the proven principles of success. But most had given up and surrendered. They were just living day to day, sadly hanging out until the bitter end.

The saddest stories are those of young people who, for whatever reason, have given up on their dreams. The young lady who once dreamed of playing volleyball at her favorite university on scholarship, but who is now working for minimum wage at a coffee house. Or the middle school boy who says, "Yeah, I'm going to play basketball at my favorite university," only to be lazily hanging out on the street corner a few years later.

But occasionally, I run across a kid who tells me some version of this: "Mr. Singletary, you wouldn't believe how much I endured to

VISUALIZE YOUR GREATNESS

get where I am. I have experienced setbacks. My friends, and even my parents, ridiculed my dream. Some days were hard, really hard. But I never concentrated on either my past failures or successes. I just took it one day at a time."

For those kids who saw their dreams fulfilled, they seized every day as a new day and prepared with purpose to meet the challenge of that one single day.

Sometimes, the people who "make it" and those who don't both have a deep commitment to putting successful habits into practice. The only difference between them is that the ones who fail postpone practicing those habits until tomorrow!

Whether we realize it or not, we are all writing a screenplay of our lives. We are all writing our own version of how we want to live. But, even if our script lays out very detailed plans for how we will rise above the life we've been given, the ending of our story will not be the one we wished for unless it includes a firm commitment to seize the opportunities of the only day we have—today. Neither yesterday nor tomorrow has any bearing on today.

The Bible says it both ways. The apostle Paul encouraged his readers to forget the past and instead "press on toward the goal" before them. Then, Jesus warned us about worrying about what *might* happen in the future when he said, "Therefore do not worry about tomorrow, for tomorrow will worry about itself. Each day has enough trouble of its own." (Matt. 6:34)

As the Roman poet Horace said two thousand years ago, "carpe diem." Seize the day. Take it captive to do your bidding to realize your dream today.

"Above all else, guard your heart, for everything you do flows from it ... " (Prov. 4:23)

PRINCIPLE 3

CONSISTENCY

---

con·sist·ent

/kən'sist(ə)nt/

adjective

... acting or done in the same way over time, especially so as to be fair or accurate.

---

1. SUCCESSFUL PEOPLE ARE ALWAYS CONSISTENTLY GROWING

At some point during my second year as a starting linebacker for the Bears, I asked Coach Buddy Ryan what it would take for me to play on the nickel defense. Buddy was an old-school coach who didn't spend a lot of his energy babysitting his players. He was gruff and direct, capable of ripping us to shreds if he felt the need for it.

VISUALIZE YOUR GREATNESS

He turned his head my way, glared at me, and without a smile, said, "Singletary, you will never play on the nickel defense." With that, he just walked away!

My obsession with playing nickel came out of a conversation I had with our PR director, Ken Valdiserri. When I asked him what it would take for me to become NFL Defensive Player of the Year, he said, "Singletary, you gotta play every down on defense. The problem is you're the middle linebacker on Buddy's defense."

Until that point in my career, most middle linebackers in the NFL would come out of the game after the second down, when the coach would send in the nickel defense.

Anyone else might have tucked their tail between their legs and walked away, but Buddy and I had one thing in common—I was as stubborn as he was. He didn't intimidate me at all. For one thing, I knew that he valued me as a player because I was starting every game. Secondly, I knew how hard I was working, so I didn't go to him with my hat in my hand, like I was begging for a few crumbs.

All during the rest of the season, I would periodically ask him the same question. "Coach, if I were to play on the nickel defense, what would I have to do?" His response was always the same. "Why are you bugging me? It's not going to happen."

At the end of the season, I approached him one more time and asked him, "Coach, I know I'm not going to play nickel linebacker, but if I were, what would I have to do?

I like to think that I amused him with my persistence. But, finally, he told me what I wanted to know.

"You can't play on nickel at your weight. You'll need to drop down to 225 pounds, like a large safety. You will also need to cover the fastest running backs, the tight ends, and sometimes receivers. At the same time, you'll need to take on those three-hundred-pound

PRINCIPLE 3: CONSISTENCY

offensive linemen. Trust me, Singletary, it ain't gonna happen. You can't do both because it's just too much thinking."

Like I said, Coach Ryan was stubborn. What he may or may not have known was that I was actually more headstrong than he was—by a mile. I wanted his approval to play every defensive down, and I wasn't going to let up until it happened.

A few days later, I went back to Baylor University to finish my degree and completely devoted myself to training to play the nickel defense. I got my weight down to 226! I ran long distances! I worked out hard in the weight room every day! I pestered Coach Ryan and relentlessly asked for more film until he told me that he had already sent me everything he had.

During that offseason, I also ran drills covering Hall of Famer Charlie Joiner of the Chargers, one of the best route runners in the league, and Darrell Green, who was a defensive back for the Redskins, who are now called the Commanders. I enlisted some of the safeties to help me, such as my roommate Todd Bell, one of my best friends on the team. Todd told me, "You'll want to cover like Willie Brown. He covers the receivers like a blanket."

I just kept working at it all during that offseason. I hit it hard! I never let up one bit.

Before, during, and after every practice, I spent some time working out with the receivers and backs, which frustrated Coach Ryan. But I didn't care! I knew what I had committed to in my mind. I wasn't going to let it go.

Early in the 1983 season, our nickel linebacker was injured. I didn't beg Coach like a little kid, "Put me in, Coach! Put me in, Coach!" I just ran off the sideline into the huddle. Buddy began cursing me, ordering me back to the sideline, but I didn't budge. The more he cursed me and ordered me to get off the field, the more I

VISUALIZE YOUR GREATNESS

yelled back at him, "Give me the call! Give me the call! You're gonna have to call a time-out!" I made the second play, and after that, I never came out of the game on third down until near the end of my career.

My single act of defiance turned out to be the best thing for my career. I wasn't trying to rebel against Coach Ryan, but I knew what I was prepared to do. I had no doubts. And the very next season, I was selected as the NFC Defensive Player of the Year. Then, in 1985 and 1988, I became NFL Defensive Player of the Year.

Up until that point, the Bears hadn't been winning a lot of games, primarily because our defense had not been performing to our full potential. When I was in the game on first and second down, I was the leader of the defense, but on third down, the nickel safety became the leader, which meant a different voice and a different way of communicating. And a different way of communicating led to a lack of consistency and, ultimately, a lack of success.

With me playing on all defensive downs, we had consistency. Offenses were notorious for confusing the defense when the nickel package was sent in. Now, there was no difference. We took that power away from the offense since our third-down personnel were the same as the first- and second-down personnel. It was unique in the NFL. No more confusing our defense.

Our gamble paid off. We finally began to win a few games. Buddy never apologized for not using me on nickel; in fact, he never brought it up, and neither did I. He did call me into his office one day and say to me, "Look, this is how it's going to work. If I send in a call and they audible, you're going to make me right by changing the call." I just said, "Yes, sir."

And that is just what I did. If a reporter asked me about a play that went sideways, I always said, "That's on me! I made a mistake!" Buddy

PRINCIPLE 3: CONSISTENCY

was teaching me to take ownership. What happened to our relationship as a result is that his trust level for me went through the roof.

One thing I didn't do was spend a lot of time thinking about how hard all of it was, even though it was very hard sometimes. In fact, sometimes it was painful, both emotionally and physically. And, yes, I would occasionally question whether or not I would ever get the opportunity to prove myself.

Even though I didn't know when or where it would happen, I truly believed that a day would come when I would be able to distinguish myself from the other linebackers on the team. Some of them were bigger than I was, and some may have even had more natural talent. If you remember, I had promised God that no one would outwork me or outprepare me.

I am convinced that it was my relentless and consistent preparation that set me up for the success I finally enjoyed. When the time came, I was ready.

Sometimes, we face challenges like this, and it can seem *too* challenging to us. However, I found it helpful to remember one fact, and that is that everyone practices something. We all have our daily habits and rituals. If you are one of those people who feels caught up in a spiral of failure, you need to know that you have habits and practices that set you up for that. The only reason that those failing habits are easy for you is that you have practiced them for so long that they have become natural to you. Practice isn't the problem—we all do that.

If I'm going to succeed, I must consistently practice the right things and practice them correctly. And I can never entertain the notion that it's time to quit practicing. We can never quit! Not ever!

What do you think would have happened to my vision of playing every defensive down in every game if I had told myself, "Mike, you've put in a lot of work. Why don't you take a week or two off from the grind? You've prepared enough! Reward yourself, and go back to your old bad habits for a few days. You can start again later! Besides, Buddy's never going to give you a shot at playing nickel anyhow."

I had already tried that strategy a time or two in my life. And every time I had tried to take a vacation from practice, it hadn't worked out well for me.

People will often ask me, "What does it take for me to become great?" What they really mean is, "What does it cost?" Coach Ryan didn't know that I was prepared to pay whatever it cost. I wanted to make sure that I would become the best middle linebacker of all time, and I was committed to doing whatever it would take.

You may have noticed a theme here—the word *consistency*. Consistency is more than a word or idea, however. It is also more than repetition in practice. Consistency is the quality of repetition that distinguishes between a good habit and a bad one.

Here's the thing, though—everyone consistently practices something. We can be consistently bad, good, great, or mediocre in our repetition. What we are talking about is the quality of what we repeat. Are my consistent practices done to become better? To become great? Or have I just become comfortable in falling short of greatness?

If it's success I'm after, all I need to change is the quality of my repetition. Of all the people I've met, there are three levels of people, and they all consistently repeat behaviors. They all make decisions that determine how their lives turn out.

- The excellent person says, "*I will!*" I will do whatever I have to do to become great; I don't care how painful it is. Then they put excellent repetition into practice that sets them up for greatness.

PRINCIPLE 3: CONSISTENCY

- The second person says, "*I want to!*" Almost everyone has the desire. However, some people want to know how much it's going to cost before they say, "I will!"

- The third person says, "*I won't!*" This is the person who has counted the cost and determined that it's too great.

Every one of us is hitting what we are aiming at. Either we believe the negative messages, or we don't. If we are caught up in the negative, we may not like what we hear, but we've just decided to go with the flow. It's easier that way. We hit the bull's eye every time. Unfortunately, the bull's eye is failure.

Do you want to know who's in control of the direction of your life? It's you. You are the one who chooses between, *I will, I want,* or *I won't.* No one else is in charge of that except you.

Sometimes I think about my earliest years and chuckle at my younger self. Being the youngest of ten kids, I might have had advantages my older siblings did not have. More than once, I heard family members and neighbors call me a mama's boy.

This often suggests that a child is spoiled, but that wasn't the case with me. Mama didn't enable me at all. She held my feet to the fire and expected me to live right. She trained me to pursue God and to listen to him. Because I was confined to the house during my early years, I was able to develop a relationship with her that was not like the relationships she had with my older siblings. Of course, she loved us all equally, but with one kid coming on the heels of another, she simply didn't have the time to devote to them in the same way she did with me.

I've already talked about the day my mother challenged me in the days after my dad left us. She didn't say it exactly like this, but it's the same challenge that Joshua gave to the young Israelite nation when they were flirting with the idea that they might be better off if they deserted their God. "If serving the Lord seems undesirable to you, then choose for yourselves this day whom you will serve." (Josh. 24:15)

Everyone chooses! No exceptions! Not choosing is choosing! Fortunately, there are only two options.

One, we can continue to be swept up in the same stream that everyone else is floating in. Just keep on going with the flow, taking whatever life dishes out. Do the same things in the same way that the rest of the crowd does. Settle! Compromise! Conform until you grow old!

Sadly, as we near the end of our lives, the only thing we will be able to say about that is, "Man, I sure had a lot of dreams when I was younger, but I hardly realized any of them. I wasted a lot of my life on nothing! I never committed to personal growth."

Or, secondly, we can choose to commit ourselves to growth that is driven by the consistent practice of living out our vision to the glory of God.

I'm not talking about waking up one day and jumping into a perfect life where all our imperfections and character flaws miraculously and immediately disappear. At least, I haven't experienced that yet. God is always revealing areas of my life that need to be conformed to the likeness of Christ.

What I committed myself to instead was a process where I am constantly surrendering my will to God's and inviting him to mold and shape me. That's what real growth is. And I expect to be asking God to grow me until the day I die. But to grow, I can't settle for the status quo—I must be committed to growth, and my ear must be tuned to the will of God.

How will we know that we are growing? That is a very good question!

You'll know that you are growing when you hear people saying things like, "You're not like everyone else! You aren't the same as you

PRINCIPLE 3: CONSISTENCY

used to be! What changed you?" That's when you'll know that your consistency is beginning to pay off.

2. CONSISTENCY CAN BE BORING— BUT IT'S ALWAYS REWARDING

"Mike, what do you do for fun?"

I enjoy having fun as much as the next guy.

I love being with my family. My wife and kids are the most important relationships I have on earth outside of the one I have with God. And being with my extended family, especially when all twenty-eight of us get together, is as fun as it gets for me.

I genuinely love to laugh. Recently, the whole family was gathered together in one house for vacation, and all of my girls and my daughter-in-law were in the corner talking … all of them chattering at the same time. It was the craziest thing I'd ever seen. I just smiled, knowing that I had been blessed more than I had thought I would be when I was a younger man.

And then there's my older son, Matt. That boy has always talked so loud that people thought he was yelling. While he's talking out loud, he's teasing us, and that level of energy makes me smile every time.

Sometimes, I just sit back and take it in. It almost overwhelms me when I think about the satisfaction I get from just having this amazing family. I find myself praying, "Father God, you have definitely been good to me. Thank you!"

I really love music—all kinds of music. Good music can energize me, inspire me, or relax me, depending on the genre.

If I have one problem with fun, however, it's that I can't just launch from a squatting position into having fun. I have to be in the right frame of mind. And I can't be in the right frame of mind if I have unfinished tasks or haven't fulfilled my responsibilities.

This is why I make lists of important things that must be done. On this list, there are two items at the top. They are the most important items because they have to do with my two most important relationships in my life. One of those is my relationship with God, and the other is the one I have with Kim.

So, I check my heart daily to see if I am living up to the expectations I have set for myself in those two areas with the following two questions.

Have I spent enough time with God?

This is number one because my relationship with him is the most important one in my life. I frequently stop what I'm doing and take stock of whether or not I have ignored a prompt from him about anything I need to take care of. He is the one I am most interested in hearing from because he is the one who has the words of life. No one else loves me like he does—not my mother, my wife, or my kids. I check myself to see if I'm paying attention to discipline in prayer and Bible reading. If not, I correct myself.

Have I spent good quality time with my wife, Kim?

This is my second most valuable relationship. I want to make sure I am paying attention to this one, for sure. Early on in our marriage, I even went as far as writing down questions to ask her—things such as, "How can I do a better job of loving you? Am I giving you and the kids the time you need and deserve? Where do you see us in five or ten years? Am I meeting your needs emotionally?"

I wrote these questions out in a checklist, in part because I did not have the best example of what a good father looked like while I was growing up. I wanted to make sure that I was the one to break the unchristlike Singletary father and husband chains that had tormented our family for far too long.

PRINCIPLE 3: CONSISTENCY

When I first began to ask Kim these questions, I had the list in my hand as I quizzed her. I actually thought to myself, "I'm quite the guy! I'm nothing like my father. Any woman would want a man who asks her questions like these."

So, I was confused when she seemed too busy to answer my questions. I was admittedly a little slow to come around, but I finally realized that it seemed to her that I was more interested in getting approval from her for just asking the questions than I was in hearing her responses. When I was finally ready to listen, she began to open up to me.

Once I started paying attention, there were times I really didn't like what she had to say, but I knew I needed to hear it. I still do! I'm open to whatever Kim has to say to me about what kind of father, husband, and follower of Christ I am because she knows me better than I know myself.

The process of consistently paying attention to these important relationships can be boring sometimes. However, sometimes, Kim's answers are uncomfortable because seeing myself as a husband from her perspective can illuminate my own flaws and failures. In my opinion and experience, nothing is more exciting than looking back over a lifetime and seeing incredible fruit grow out of taking care of the boring and uncomfortable things.

I don't know if you could call all of this fun, like bungee jumping would be fun to some people. There isn't always an adrenaline rush, but it's fun in the sense that I can look back over the years with incredible joy and satisfaction, knowing that I have dedicated myself to consistently nurturing these relationships.

And that is my point about consistency. If we are going to finally enjoy our vision, our journey there must be intentional. I find that when I have taken care of the boring details, when I have consistently prepared to live out my vision, I can fully enjoy the lighter moments because I am free of the nagging feeling that I've left something truly important undone.

3. CONSISTENTLY APPLY THE B-WE-H FORMULA

I've been incredibly fortunate to meet a lot of great people in my life. Whenever I get the opportunity, I ask them what led to their success. They may not have heard of my B-WE-H formula, but almost all of them have followed it.

Belief

Rarely do I meet successful people who say, "I never saw that coming. I didn't expect to be successful; it just happened." And when I say "rarely," I mean almost never.

The vast majority of successful people have one thing in common: They all had a plan, a vision. They thought about their vision constantly, even dreamed about it. They believed that their vision would become real. They studied others who were successful in practicing their craft and leaned on their wisdom. They trained their minds to think about all of this.

Before I ever wrote out my vision when I was twelve years old, I had to believe that it was meant for me, that it was something that I would sacrifice for. Without a fervent belief that you can actually accomplish what you've set your mind to, it's almost impossible to move forward.

Work Ethic

Unfortunately, our culture has done such a good job of robbing us of our work ethic that a lot of people don't even have any idea what it is. In fact, we might have to go back several generations to find an ancestor who even possessed it.

PRINCIPLE 3: CONSISTENCY

However, it's not complicated. In fact, it's very simple—*work ethic is the belief that it is a privilege to work hard and the confident knowledge that good will result from giving your best effort to everything you do.*

Work ethic is putting our belief in our dream into practice, allowing it to become our vision, and never backing away from it.

Humility

Humility is the final piece of the B-WE-H principle that truly successful people practice.

Humility isn't the same as hanging your head in shame and endlessly beating yourself with a whip. Instead, it is living with the awareness that whatever you accomplish was not accomplished alone. I don't care who you are; there were teachers, friends, mentors, and experts in your life who helped you to become successful. Humble people never forget this.

Humility is also knowing that you don't deserve anything. You aren't entitled.

Instead, humility says, "If I don't prepare, I will not win! If I am unwilling to learn from others, I will fall flat on my face! I'm not nearly as awesome as I am tempted to think I am!"

During the 1989 season with the Bears, I was taught a valuable lesson about humility. We were 4–0, and I was on fire. After win number four, I was bragging to my teammate Richard Dent that, in all the time I had played linebacker, no one had ever run over me. Not even once!

The very next game, we played the Buccaneers at home. It was the final seconds of the game, and we were ahead by a couple of points. I gathered the defense together, gave them the play, and said, "Don't try to tackle the receiver! Just keep him in bounds."

The quarterback threw the ball to their running back, James Wilder. I just stood there flat-footed, assuming that Wilder would run out of bounds to stop the clock. Instead, he turned his shoulders, squared me up, and ran right through me. I jumped up quickly, but it was too late. The damage had been done. Someone else made the tackle, but he had already gotten close enough for the Buccaneers to kick a game-winning field goal.

I was stunned. I had to eat my words. I learned a valuable lesson that day: *Keep your mouth closed, Singletary!*

It was true that I was on the field that day, in part because I had prepared to be there, but I was also there because I had several people in my corner cheering me on, rebuking my tendency to settle for mediocrity, and encouraging me when I was down. Not only that, but God had been my guide since day one. Unfortunately, for a brief moment, I had forgotten all of that. I had thought it was all about Mike Singletary. I had believed what the fans had been saying about me.

God has a way of exposing our pride when we forget where we came from and who helped us get there. I should have remembered that.

4. CONSISTENTLY BE PREDICTABLE

I'm a fairly predictable guy. I don't often fly by the seat of my pants. I always do things a certain way, and very rarely do I vary from my routines and preferences. For example, I have always been the first to show up on the job and am often the last to leave. If I'm in the presence of a lady, I'll treat her with respect.

I'm also completely predictable about food. For one thing, I don't do potlucks very well because I'm never really sure who prepared the dishes.

PRINCIPLE 3: CONSISTENCY

I like things a certain way. If Kim prepares a pot of pinto beans for dinner, it must be accompanied by corn bread. If there's none there, I'm more than happy to run to Trader Joe's and buy some. I'll even make it if I have to.

My obsession with food is elevated when it comes to holiday meals. I love Thanksgiving stuffing, for example, but I simply can't eat it without a mess of candied yams on the side of the plate.

Early on in our marriage, Kim was preparing stuffing for the holiday meal, and while she was laboring over the pots and pans, I suggested she contact my mom to find out how she made it. I loved my mom's stuffing.

Bad move! I didn't make that mistake twice!

I've always thought of my predictability as one of my greatest strengths. And while it's true that being predictable in my habits and practices has served me well over the years, there's a fine line between predictability and inflexibility.

The difference between the two is that inflexibility is self-focused. It's about me and what I want. It doesn't take others into consideration. I've worked hard to submit to God in this area.

Predictably choosing to practice good habits by submitting to God in every area of my life is something I will be committed to for the rest of my life. In fact, I plan on being more predictable in those areas as I get older, because when I'm predictably practicing good habits, I know that I'm also choosing God's version of the good life instead of my own flawed version.

5. CONSISTENTLY TAKE CARE OF YOURSELF

After I retired from the Bears, I took a break from football for about ten years. During that time, I traveled to speaking engagements in

VISUALIZE YOUR GREATNESS

other parts of the country about four or five times a month. I also did a little corporate consulting, but most of the time, I worked from home. I chose this work schedule because it allowed me to spend more time with Kim and our seven children.

When I finally began coaching, I spent some time in Baltimore as a linebacker coach. I soon found out that the NFL took the health of its coaches as seriously as it did that of the players. Not very long after I arrived in Baltimore, the team doctor called me one day and said, "Coach, it's time for your physical."

I hadn't visited the doctor since I had retired from playing. Truthfully, I was thinking that my physical would be a slam dunk. I was only ten pounds over my playing weight, and I worked out several times a week. I lived a relatively low-stress life. So, I was completely confident that the doctor would say, "You're all good to go, Coach. Just keep on doing what you're doing."

Instead, he sat me down and asked a couple of questions that had me a little concerned.

"Do you have any history of diabetes in your family, Mike? Any history of high blood pressure?"

I told him that I did.

He leaned over his desk a bit, looked me in the eye, and said, "Well, your test results are OK, but if you keep doing what you're doing, you'll have both of those things."

We talked at length about how I needed to lose weight, even more than the ten pounds I had put on since I had quit football. He counseled me about the hidden sugars and salts in food, especially restaurant food.

I made a decision right then and there that our family was going to change its habits when it came to our diet. I stopped at a bookstore on the way home and bought a couple of books on nutrition. Kim and I had never been big on eating out. When you have seven kids, eating in a restaurant always becomes an ordeal. After we committed to our dietary changes, we agreed that we wouldn't trust public eating places for our main source of nutrition.

In that doctor's office, I realized that all of my hard work to live the good life could be cut short if I continued to endanger my health and the health of my family.

6. CONSISTENTLY LOOK FOR THE GOOD

I wasn't built to play middle linebacker like some of the other guys in the league were. I wasn't as tall, and I didn't jump as high, and I wasn't as strong as most of them.

Years before I committed myself to football, I was preparing to play. I just didn't know that's what I was doing.

In my dad's construction business, all my brothers and I were required to help. It was hot, dirty, grueling work. My brothers all learned construction skills, but I had no interest in that, so I was given the grunt work to do—digging, shoveling, swinging a sledgehammer, leveling poured driveways, and picking up nails.

Once my mother gave me permission to play organized football, I was excited to be hitting other players instead of concrete. While the other guys were complaining about the heat, the long hours, and the hard work, I was just happy to be sweating and working hard at something I loved.

It was years before I realized just how much my dad had prepared me to be successful in sports, even though he would never have let me play if he'd stuck around.

I had hated him all that time because he was such a hard man to love. For the longest time, when I thought of my father, all that I could remember about him were his outbursts of anger, his cursing, and his cruelty.

After a few years passed, however, I was able to take a step back and dig through the dirt of my relationship with him and search for something good. And what I found was this nugget of gold that was the foundation of my success in sports. He instilled a strong work ethic in me, and he taught me to pay attention to details and finish a job with excellence.

I now know that my dad loved us, but it would have been nice to hear him say a time or two, "Son, I'm proud of you. I love you!"

Sadly, he was incapable of that because no one had done that for him. He had no context for affection or intimacy, but he did give me the only thing he could. He gifted me with a desire to succeed no matter how high the temporary costs were.

The point is that little nugget was there all along. I just didn't see it until I began to peel back the layers of our relationship and look for it. I've sometimes wondered how different our relationship would have been had I been able to look past his obvious painful flaws and see something good.

What I've learned is that no one is 100 percent bad. Even the most wicked person in the history of the world probably had at least one redeeming quality. The reverse is also true: No one is 100 percent good either. I know this is true about me. I want to be good. I even try to be good. The truth is, sometimes, I'm not that good.

Looking for good in others isn't the same as rubber-stamping approval for what they do wrong. I certainly don't agree with the harm my father caused to our family. I just know that I would have never been able to move on from all of that if I hadn't at least considered the possibility that my dad had at least one redeeming quality. I believe my dad was special. But he, like the rest of us, just needed to learn

PRINCIPLE 3: CONSISTENCY

the power of forgiveness and the value of release from forgiving others who hurt us, and even more importantly, from forgiving ourselves.

7. CONSISTENTLY BE AWARE THAT NOT EVERYONE ELSE IS OK

Here's where the rubber meets the road for me. If I think that success is what I accomplish and accumulate for my own glory and comfort, then I've missed the boat. Self-promotion and self-gratification are idols that will rob me of my joy and purpose.

The person who is truly successful is the one who looks outside themselves and asks, "Who can I help today? How can I use what God has given me to help someone else?" I don't mean just acknowledging the pain and suffering of others. I'm talking about my intentional intervention into the brokenness of other people's lives. How can I really help them?

What I have discovered by opening my eyes and heart a little is that a lot of us are in the throes of what is now called a *mental health crisis*. This is a new term, but honestly, humanity has suffered from broken hearts and dreams, from hopelessness and despair, since creation. It's really not new at all.

Still, it seems to me to be getting worse. Suicides are up! Addictions and overdoses are up! The same false promises that Mr. Johnson sold in his liquor store in Sunnyside when I was a kid are being mass-marketed today by bars, nightclubs, and drug dealers. Wall Street has become really good at convincing us that the good life can be enjoyed just by purchasing more of what it is selling.

Unfortunately, none of the promises that the world makes ever deliver. And when we have invested everything that we have, chasing our tails, we sooner or later wake up to realize that we've run after things that will never satisfy us. In fact, most of them will destroy us along with our dreams of a better life.

It's more than OK to be OK with noticing that not everyone is OK—we are all in this together. I can't truly be successful until I notice the suffering of others and draw them into a friendship that is supportive and helps carry some of their pain. After all, this is exactly what others have done for me.

The problem is that I can't lead people where I haven't been. God has used others to teach me that it's also OK for me to be open about the stresses and failures in my own life. He has taught me (and he's still teaching me) that holding in that kind of garbage only increases the levels of the stress hormones cortisol and adrenaline in my body. I have to let it out. Sometimes, I just confess it to Kim or my friend Ron first. Kim usually reminds me that we need to pray about it.

As bad as cortisol and adrenaline are, God has created us with the ability to release two other hormones that neutralize them. How amazing is it that dopamine and serotonin are both released when we let others share our burdens and when we pray, especially when our prayer is centered on the faithfulness and goodness of God? It's hard to stand before him, soak up his majesty and love and his affection for us, and then turn around and continue to let the junk of the world eat away at our insides.

Even something simple, such as distancing ourselves from the distractions of our devices, getting out in the sunlight, exercising, or eating healthy foods, increases these pleasure hormones. And we need them.

None of us is OK 100 percent of the time—not you and not me.

That's why practicing good mental health habits is so important. Luckily, I had an excellent role model for this: my mother.

PRINCIPLE 3: CONSISTENCY

Time and time again, after seeing my mother argue with my father over things like whether we would have enough money to pay the bills, or even have supper that evening, I can remember her pinning laundry on the clothesline, looking up into the sky and saying with a smile, "Wow, ain't God good."

Taking small moments of intentional gratitude for our Creator and his creation are some of the healthiest habits you can have. When I do that, then I can lend a hand to people for whom not everything is OK, people who may be battling depression, for example. Maybe they're even struggling with an addiction that began when they decided to self-medicate with drugs or alcohol.

All I know is that I want to consistently be aware of the people God has put in my life who are not OK.

PRINCIPLE 4
CONFIDENT

---

con·fi·dence

/ˈkänfəd(ə)ns/

noun

the feeling or belief that one can rely on someone or something; firm trust.

---

1. HOW CAN I BE CONFIDENT?

Getting a job coaching was usually fairly easy for me. Everyone knew of my passion and commitment to preparation. The coaches and front office staff also knew that I understood defense as well as anyone. So, once I put my hat in the ring, the word got around: "Mike Singletary wants to coach."

As I said, the first few jobs came easily enough. It was as simple as getting a phone call, and the coach or general manager would say something like, "Mike, we need you here. When can you start?"

VISUALIZE YOUR GREATNESS

But then an opportunity came to apply for a position with a team that was coached by a guy I knew. The only thing different that time was that I would have to sit for an interview. I had never done that before.

Before I walked into the conference room on the day of my interview, I thought I had prepared myself. I had studied the team film, and I had quizzed a few of their coaches and players whom I already knew about their defense. Not only that, but several of the assistant coaches and players had called me to express their excitement about the possibility of me joining the team.

I arrived for the interview thinking, *I've got this thing wrapped up! I've got this job in the bag.*

Not long after the interview began, however, the defensive coordinator leaned back in his plush office chair, put his ten fingers together in front of his face, and said, "OK, Mike, draw up this defense—*under saw one funnel.*"

I don't want to get all in the weeds about what that is, except to say that I was dumbfounded. I knew what an *under saw one* defense was, but I had no idea what *funnel* meant here. That term was used so rarely in the circles I was in that I had only heard it one or two times in all the years I was in the NFL.

My response did not instill confidence in the minds of my interviewers. I stumbled, stuttered, and made a complete fool of myself. If I had been truly prepared, and if I had truly had confidence in myself, I would have said, "I'm not familiar with that term, but here's what a *under saw one* defense looks like," and then drawn it on the whiteboard.

I felt unprepared. I also felt like I had been sabotaged, and as soon as I dejectedly returned to my car after the "interview," I told God as much.

"Why did you let me get my hopes up only to have this coach jerk the rug out from under me?"

As soon as the words left my mouth, I heard God speak to my heart and mind. "Don't blame me! And don't blame that coach! You are the one who didn't prepare. You are the one who let one word sabotage your interview. It's all on you, Mike!"

Was I confident entering the interview? I'd thought I was. But in retrospect, I would have to admit that I wasn't. But I was cocky! They aren't the same thing! To be honest, I was thinking, *I'm Mike Singletary, Hall of Famer! Look at what I've done with linebackers! I've coached two Hall of Famers in Patrick Willis and Ray Lewis. I'm sure there are some others I've coached who will be in the Hall of Fame as well. I shouldn't have to prove myself in a conference room.*

My expectation going in was that they would say, "These are the defenses that we run, and here are the techniques that you would need to teach, and these are the linebackers we have. When can you start?"

Like all the other times God has disciplined me, his chastisement did not (as the Bible says) seem pleasant at the time. But looking back on it, I am grateful for the humiliation now because it was one of those moments that shaped me a little bit more into the man I had begged God to make out of me all those years ago.

And that is what the Word of God says—that the unpleasantness of discipline later produces a harvest of righteousness and peace. Another way of saying that is that you can't experience real inner peace until you've been disciplined and trained by God.

After the smoke cleared from my disastrous interview, I began to ask myself what I could have done differently. What God told me is that I could have prepared by asking more questions of the coaches and players from that team, such as, "Is there any special language the coach uses that I might not be aware of? Any unique terms?"

But even if I had not done that, I should have asked advice from others about how a proper interview is conducted. I should have been prepared for trick questions. I would have sailed through the interview had I just admitted my ignorance of that one word and gone on to draw up the formation on the board.

The bottom line? My confidence was based on the wrong fundamentals. As a result, my goose was already cooked as soon as I walked into that room because I had failed to prepare.

2. WHY DO SO MANY PEOPLE LACK CONFIDENCE?

I was raised in a home centered on the Word of God: the Bible. My dad was a pastor, and as I've already said, he was an expert at using the Bible to beat people over the head. I certainly did not learn my love for the wisdom of God from him. In fact, he almost sabotaged my faith when I was younger because of the hypocrisy I saw in him.

But my mother? In a way, I hate to keep bringing her into my story, but I wouldn't even have a story if not for her. I have met very few people like her. Her devotion to God and the written Word of God was unparalleled. She was definitely one of a kind.

Despite all the hell that surrounded her—the abuse from my father, her other broken children who had been destroyed by my dad, the poverty, and the loss of two of her precious kids—she never wavered in her faith in the goodness of God.

By the time I came along, I was five years younger than the next youngest sibling, so she had time to mentor me in a way that she had been unable to do with the rest of her kids. And then, after my father left, he wasn't there to try to undo the good she was doing in my life.

PRINCIPLE 4: CONFIDENT

Once he had left, my mother was able to turn on the afterburners with me.

She was a hard worker during the day, but by the time the sun went down every night, all her attention was focused on training me to embrace God's purposes. She told me about God's abundant promises. She told me about the story in Genesis of how God honored and blessed Joseph, who was faithful even when no one else was. I learned from her that God always keeps his promises to those who faithfully pursue him.

Once I became aware of God's goodness, she nurtured in me an unshakable faith that if I walked with Christ, then there would be no dream too big for God. I learned from her example and began to believe that, despite the abuse and the generational poverty we lived in, I too could be raised above all of that and live with an unquenchable desire for the approval of God.

Hour after hour and day after day, she made certain that I knew God's love. I don't mean that I knew "about" his love, but that she made sure that I experienced it, that I lived every day conscious of the love and goodness of my Heavenly Father.

To be honest, I had everything going against me. I was too sick, too skinny, too short, and too slow to play middle linebacker. Not only that, but I was also full of fear, too afraid to dream of something that everything and everyone in my life said was beyond my abilities. But I had a secret weapon! My strength came from repeating the promises of God—*he loves me, and I can do all things through him.*

I know that my circumstances were not unique. I don't know how many kids have grown up in neighborhoods like Sunnyside over the years or had a father who left them, but I do know that there were only a couple of my peers who believed that something else besides what we had been raised in was possible. Just two or three, that's all.

But would you like to know what we all had in common? Each of us had someone who uplifted us and told us that we were loved by God, that he even liked us and would hold our trembling hands as we pursued our dreams.

My mother had a vision, not only for her life but for mine as well. And even though she never said it this way, I think she would agree that a vision that isn't generational is not a vision but simply a good idea.

This is why I've tried to live my life this way. Not only has God gifted me with a vision and the strength to live it out, but he has convinced me that my vision is incomplete if I don't pass it on. I need to look for others with whom I can share it.

I've tried to share it with my kids in the same way my mother did with me. And there are others too—kids (and even some adults) who come from the Sunnysides of America—from the hoods, the Native American reservations, the poverty-stricken areas of Appalachia, and even the affluent neighborhoods where it's easy to conceal our frustrations with our own personal failures behind excessive materialism.

So, in answer to why people don't have real confidence to live out their lives with meaning, I think it boils down to this: They are living in ignorance! They don't know that almost everything they learn from the world about how to live purposefully is just not true.

I don't blame them. They don't have the secret sauce. I say secret sauce, but it's not really that big of a secret if you're looking for it. The Bible says that confidence comes from knowing that God, "who began a good work" in me, "will carry it on to completion until the day of Christ." That's it in a nutshell. God wants to work in us to develop us and grow us.

We may be confident in our abilities in one area of our lives or another—sports, or investing in securities, or repairing an automobile—but the kind of confidence I'm talking about is the thought that we wake up with every day that says, *I know why I'm here. I know my purpose. I know what God wants from me!* There is no greater confidence than to know that God is on our side and guiding our development.

And guess what! This is something I pursue and prepare for in the same way I prepared to be confident in football. Only, the stakes are much higher and the reward more fulfilling when I seek God. I think I was pretty good at playing football, but those days are long behind me. I'll never play another down. But knowing that God began a good work in me, and that he will keep on doing that work until he's finished, is something that will last forever.

This kind of confidence will change how I play sports or how well I do my job at McDonald's. It will change how I lead my family and love my wife, but it's bigger than even those things. It's knowing that I walk with God because he's walking with me. Not only that, but he's also empowering me to dream big dreams, dreams no one thought were possible.

3. HOW DO WE LOSE CONFIDENCE?

The easy answer is that we forget whom we belong to, and we stop pursuing him and his wisdom. That's how we lose confidence.

Remember when I told you about my early dreams, where I imagined that I would hold my kids in my lap, play with them on the floor, and tell them repeatedly that I loved them?

Man, did I have it all worked out or what? I thought I had a plan to be an awesome parent. My kids would adore me, and my wife would stand back in awe of my impressive skills as a dad. I honestly thought that I would show her how it's done.

My problem was, however, that I didn't have a real plan at all. The only strategy I had was to look at my father and do the opposite. I will confess that I came up with that strategy long before I met Kim. But she came from a much different kind of family from mine, so she was far better prepared to be a mom than I was to be a dad.

So, when our first child, Kristen, was born on Father's Day, I took that as a sign that God had rubber-stamped my strategy for raising kids. And to be honest, she was an easy child to raise. She smiled at everyone she met, and she ate well, and she grew in sync with expectations on the growth charts.

The same was true with Matt, who was born a year and a half later. I thought, *Man, I'm killing this fatherhood thing*. Kim was a stay-at-home mom, but I secretly took responsibility for how awesome our kids were.

But as more children came along, my confidence in my fatherhood began to take a beating. I started out this daddy thing wanting to run a tight ship. There would be no foolishness in my house. So, when one of them would whimper or cry or fuss, I took it as a personal challenge to my belief that I was an incredible dad. I wanted to take their little faces in my hands and firmly remind them, "We can't have this! Not in my house!"

I am so thankful for Kim, who was far more experienced and realistic about kids and how to raise them. She would calmly reassure me, "It's OK, Baby! She's just teething!" or "Her tummy is upset! She'll be OK!" She knew that what I had taken as a challenge to my position as the father of the house was just run-of-the-mill baby stuff.

Because no one had modeled good fatherhood to me, I was woefully unprepared to be a dad. As it turned out, I had no realistic foundation for my confidence that I would be a good parent. A bunch of what I thought a good dad looked like was pipe-dream stuff.

PRINCIPLE 4: CONFIDENT

It's true that I was a far better dad than my own father had been. No doubt about that. But I was a little slow coming around to the fact that just being better than my very flawed father was not nearly good enough. My kids deserved a father who was a great dad.

I could have given up and told myself the same lie I'd heard growing up in the hood. "You're no good at this daddy thing! You might as well not even try! Just give up!"

However, that was not an option for me because of the promise I had made to God when I was thirteen years old: "I will give my best to everything you put before me." And now, I had a job to do that was of far more importance than anything else. Nothing else mattered to me compared to my love for Kim and the kids. It wasn't even close.

I had lost confidence in my ability to be a dad because my expectations were all out of kilter. My "confidence" was a mile wide and an inch deep. As it turns out, I wasn't really confident at all. But once again, I was arrogant. I thought I already knew what it meant to be a great dad, so I didn't really ask God what it meant, nor did I go to the great fathers I knew to get their advice. I didn't ask Kim either. I just went with my plan, which, admittedly, was very flawed.

But when I finally confessed my own shortcomings in this one area of my life and realized that God had been modeling good fatherhood to me for a long time, I began to try to imitate him. After all, the Bible says that, when we turn to God and he gives us his Spirit to live in us, we are able to see him as *Abba*. Abba means "daddy" in Aramaic, and it suggests an even more intimate relationship. God had been my one and only father from the time my mother conceived me in her womb.

The lesson for me was unmistakably clear. The only way I could ever know what it means to be a good father was to look at my Heavenly Father, my Abba.

I had failed at all of that! However, I had also learned that failure is never permanent unless we stay in the dirt after getting knocked down. I was successful at being a pretty good dad, but I wanted to be a great one, so I stood up, shook the dust off me, and submitted to God's perfect example of fatherhood. When I felt him urging me to change something in my approach to parenting, I did it. On the spot. I didn't hesitate or negotiate. I just obeyed.

My Heavenly Father taught me to be a better dad, that's for sure, but he also taught me how to be a better husband, employee, citizen, and church member. As I saw him more and more as the father I never had, my imitation of him transformed me.

When I see my life as a masterpiece being painted by the master artist, there's never a time when surrender is an option. Even when I stumble, I take it for what it is—God is still doing something in me that isn't yet complete. This is why I can live confidently, even in light of my mistakes and miscues. God's still working! It's not about me—it's about him.

4. CONFIDENCE VERSUS PRIDE AND ARROGANCE

While I was coaching the 49ers in San Francisco, we prepared to face the Tampa Bay Buccaneers midway through the season. The entire team was confident that it would be an easy win for us, partly because Tampa Bay wasn't having a good year and partly because I was confident. The entire team followed my lead.

We weren't in the game long before I noticed that we were down 25–0. I couldn't believe that my well-prepared team was losing by twenty-five points, and to Tampa Bay of all teams. It didn't matter what we did; they seemed to have an answer to every one of our offensive downs.

PRINCIPLE 4: CONFIDENT

I must admit, I was baffled, even dumbfounded. We had the right personnel and what I thought was a fantastic game plan, but instead of dominating them as I had expected, we were the ones being dominated.

After the game ended, we left confused and with our tails between our legs. Some of my coaches went out for dinner with one of Tampa Bay's assistant coaches, and he spilled the beans. They had relentlessly studied game film and discovered a "tell" that our running back gave that told them exactly what we were going to do.

I must hand it to them—it was a brilliant move on their part.

Going into the game, we thought we were confident. But it wasn't really confidence that we had. Actually, we were entitled. As a result of Tampa Bay's disciplined study of game film, despite their dismal record that year, they were more confident than we were. They knew they would win the game long before the coin toss because they had found our Achilles' heel. And when you know your opponent's weakness and have a plan to exploit it, it generates measurable excitement within your team.

I should have known better. I have already told you how, as a player, I studied so much game film that I could often call out the play that the opposing offense was going to run before their quarterback did. I couldn't wait for the opposition to snap the ball.

Unfortunately for me and my team, it hadn't occurred to me that I should have continued to watch film as a coach in the same way I had as a player. It hurt me when I found out that Tampa Bay had done to me what I once did to the teams I played against when I was with the Bears.

I learned my lesson that day and began to prepare for games as a coach in the same way that I did as a player. I also learned that this is the difference between confidence and pride. Confidence is deeply rooted in the substance of preparation. Pride has a surface-level base. Pride listens to what others are saying about our greatness. Pride comes when we believe our own press. But that kind of greatness is usually short-lived.

Greatness isn't about our natural talents as much as it is about this kind of preparation. It requires gaining the competitive edge. It's looking in the mirror at the end of the day and asking yourself, "Have you done everything you could possibly do today to win?" and answering, "Yes! Yes, I did!" That's confidence.

Not to repeat myself too much, but greatness also means that, even when you fail, you get up, dust yourself off, and run back into the game. Even when everything in you tells you to throw in the towel, you refuse to do so. Instead, you prepare harder.

The bottom line is that doing anything less than our best is not going to make us confident. Confidence is saying, "I gave it my all, so tomorrow belongs to me!"

5. CONFIDENCE SHINES THROUGH WHEN YOUR PLAN ISN'T WORKING

Would you like to know how to find out what you're made of? It's when you get hit in the mouth by life. When you lose the game, or your boyfriend dumps you, or the scholarship goes to someone else. You find out when you're short on cash and are forced to either pay the light bill or buy groceries.

This is when you have a choice to make. And how you choose will make all the difference in the world. Do you close shop, pack up everything, and start blaming others? Do you blame your failure on the system that is rigged against you? Do you wallow in self-pity?

Trust me! I've been there and found it to be a very lonely place. But it was in that place of failure that God spoke to me and commanded

PRINCIPLE 4: CONFIDENT

me to stand up like a man and trust his plan for my life. I sensed that he was telling me, "OK, enough of the pity party. That won't get you anywhere! Now, get back to work on the things that will get you out of this mess." Often, that involved simply turning around and heading in the opposite direction.

This is what I did when I was faced with failure. I chose to listen to God instead of all the other chatter that had gotten me nowhere.

6. CONFIDENCE IN THE FACE OF FEAR

Remember when I told you about how I wrote down my vision and nailed it to the wall of my bedroom after my dad deserted us? Well, I would like to say that I boldly wrote out my vision without any fear at all.

But, apparently, that's not true. For one thing, I can't remember how many versions of my vision I penned only to wad the paper up and toss it on the floor. And even later, there were occasions when I would grow frustrated with my progress, tear my vision paper from where it was stapled, and rip it into shreds, only to write it again and post it to the wall once more.

It was often hard because the nagging feeling of fear kept creeping back into my mind, and it threatened to derail my plans. I'm not exaggerating here—in the beginning, I had almost no encouragement to pursue my vision from anyone other than my mom. Aunts and uncles reminded me how this cousin or that aunt had tried to escape the poverty of Sunnyside only to fail. Even my own siblings thought my dream was silly.

Was I afraid? Well, yes! I was sometimes! When you have a desire, a dream for something greater, but every example you have before you tells you that it's impossible, it's hard to see the forest for the trees.

VISUALIZE YOUR GREATNESS

I'm telling you—it was like a chorus of naysayers shouting in unison, "You silly boy! This is a stupid pipe dream! It's not going to happen!"

I have no way of knowing what voices of defeat you are hearing right now. Maybe your marriage is in the midst of a raging storm, or your children are flirting with going down the wrong path, or your business is in trouble, and every voice in your head tells you that you should just throw up the white flag of surrender.

All I know is that our subconscious thoughts are reinforced by these circumstances, and they prepare us for the soft crash landing. The subconscious collects every fear, every failure, every rejection, and every setback, and reinforces them with the thought that the change we desire is too big for us.

What I also know is that if I am not dead set on "getting out" of the doldrums of life, I won't. If I seek an easy way out, I won't prosper. To do that, I must take action. I will have to tell my subconscious, "Thanks, but I've got this." Then I must write out what I have imagined and repeat it to myself over and over until I have retrained my subconscious to see that my potential for living a good life is a greater reality than my fears tried to convince me was possible.

I must intentionally reject the lies that tell me I'm a fool for dreaming.

7. CONFIDENT PEOPLE ARE PROACTIVE

I alluded to this earlier, but if you had known me back when I was a young boy, you would hardly recognize me now. Because of my place in the birth order of the Singletary family, and because of my frequent illnesses, I was a bit of a mama's boy. I didn't have a lot of friends, so I learned to entertain myself. I didn't realize it at the time, but now

PRINCIPLE 4: CONFIDENT

I see that what I really wanted was to become invisible. It was safer for me that way.

I worked hard at being unnoticed. I had heard what others said about me: "What's wrong with that boy? Is he dull minded? Is he not right?" So, when my father left just as I was entering puberty, those thoughts were reinforced even more. If I'd had any doubts before, his departure confirmed them. He convinced me of what I had suspected: I was the last of a really bad litter.

I suppose all of this made me an easy mark for the bullies. I often had my lunch money taken from me in the elementary school shakedown. After one of these encounters, I came home bruised and bloodied. My brother Grady asked me what had happened to me, so I told him. His response frightened me.

"Get up! You're coming with me!"

"What? Wait! Where are we going?" I responded.

"We're going to find those guys, and you are going to fight them. And you'd better win, or you'll have to fight me!"

When we arrived at the school, I knew exactly where my tormentors were. But there was no way I was going to lead Grady to them, so I escorted him in the opposite direction. I wasn't about to fight that guy again and be embarrassed. And I especially didn't want to lose and duke it out with Grady either.

It's a little embarrassing now, but at the time, I was still sucking my thumb, even though my brother Charles had made it his ambition to break me of the habit. In fact, he was relentless about it—taping my thumb, coating it with jalapeño pepper sauce, and even sneaking up behind me and slapping me on the head when he caught me in the act.

Just a timid little boy, afraid of his own shadow. There was no way I was going to stand up to the bullies. I knew I would lose.

VISUALIZE YOUR GREATNESS

Nothing changed until just after my brother Grady's funeral, when my mother challenged me to become a man. Within only six months, I stopped sucking my thumb. I no longer saw myself as the runt of the litter. I no longer desired to be invisible. I became a man. I was no longer afraid!

I also separated myself (at my mom's "urging") from my four "friends" whom I had latched onto as some sort of personal protection detail. I had known they were headed for trouble, but I was tired of being bullied. I thought I needed them to fight my battles for me. As it turned out, cutting ties with them was a good move because every one of them either died young or went to prison.

There's one more lesson I learned as I began to accept the responsibilities of manhood: Those tough guys were just as insecure as I was. The only difference was that I masked my insecurity with timidity, while they masked theirs with their bravado.

So, all of this led me to take life by the horns. Instead of waiting for someone to do something for me or for good things to come my way by chance, I began to prepare to live a manly life. I observed people and the choices they were making. And I don't just mean the people who were successful; I also looked at those who were not.

I wanted to imitate the people who were "making it," but I also wanted to avoid the habits of those who were not. I even noticed that some people had everything it took to be great, but they never were because the personal cost of success was too high. Or perhaps it was because they thought if it was good enough for their dads or their uncles, it would be good enough for them. Others, like me, had no business dreaming of greatness but somehow achieved it by the grace of God.

The result of all of this was that I began to see myself not as a victim, but as a young man who had as much opportunity as anyone

100

else to live out his dream. I kind of chuckle about it now, but I recall standing shirtless before the mirror in my room, flexing my little developing muscles while repeating over and over, "I am Mike Singletary! I will be great! I will be strong! I am smart! I am not afraid of anyone or anything! I am the man of the house! Anything that happens here has to go through me! I am a child of God! I will honor him!"

Then I would turn away from the mirror and once again look at my vision posted on my wall, repeating each of the points slowly.

And, finally, I would get on my knees and plead with God to give me the strength to honor him by being faithful and relentless in pursuit of the dream he had given me.

I'm not going to lie—it was often difficult to keep the dream alive. With all the obstacles I faced, it even seemed impossible from time to time. I felt like a fraud sometimes because my dream was so unrealistic in the minds of everyone I knew. But even though I was sometimes tempted to surrender, I did not entertain that thought for long. Instead, I pursued my dream harder, more tenaciously. I changed my diet. I sought out the few people who shared my desire for a better life to study and hang out with them. I sought the counsel of strong men such as Coach Brown, who believed in me.

All of this is to say that I did not wait for good things to happen; rather, I was proactive in preparing for them to happen. And I stopped thinking, *What if these things happen?* and began to think about *when* they would happen. And somewhere along the way, I heard some advice that I've tried to live by ever since: Right decisions produce positive actions, and positive actions produce desired results.

If you are floundering in a sea of failure, it's a very easy thing to stay there. You don't have to try too hard. But you also don't have to stay there. The way back to shore is simple, but it isn't easy. Be

VISUALIZE YOUR GREATNESS

proactive! Tell yourself the direction you want your life to go in, speak it out loud, write it down, and then keep repeating it and reinforcing it with appropriate actions. Close your eyes, and see yourself doing it in your mind's eye.

Before long, you'll wake up one day and say, "Wow! I made it! Thank God, I made it!"

PRINCIPLE 5
CHARACTER

---

char·ac·ter

/ˈker(ə)ktər/

noun

the mental and moral qualities distinctive to an individual.
"running away was not in keeping with her character"

Whoever walks in integrity walks securely, but whoever takes crooked paths will be found out. (Prov. 10:9)

> *Character is the me I see, and when I stand before God I'm totally free.*
> *Personality is the side of me I want others to see,*
> *When the lights are on me.*
> *Reputation is others' opinions of me,*
> *Which they may have heard, but did not see.*
> *Through the years I've seen many rise, and even more fall,*
> *But those without character—they couldn't complete the call.*

1. WITHOUT CHARACTER, IT'S ONLY A MATTER OF TIME BEFORE YOUR TRUE SELF IS EXPOSED

Everyone has a brand of themselves, an image that they want to project to the people who know them. For example, your daughter's history teacher may want her students to see her either as loving and nurturing or as a hard-line woman who won't tolerate any foolishness in the classroom. Your pastor may project an image of himself as a righteous man who always does and says the right thing.

This is not the same thing as character. Instead, all that stuff is nothing more than a version of ourselves that we have crafted for others to see. Not the same thing! Not at all!

Character is far different from image. It is what we are when it's just us, all by ourselves. Real character flows out of our desires and our vision. If our desires are for the temporary things of the world, things such as money, sex, power, or approval, then that's what we will feed.

However, if we imagine that we are in community with the God who created us, we will find ways to feed that desire above all else. We will learn to trust that he's telling us the truth about everything.

Either way, everyone has some kind of character, either good or bad. No one is characterless. And the funny thing about character is that it is impossible to hide forever. Sooner or later, our secret character will become our public character.

I learned at a very early age that character is impossible to conceal by seeing my father manage his public image. For years, on the surface of things, many people admired him, even longed to be like him. Some even wished they had a dad like him.

How I have often wished that, for the sake of his marriage and family, Charles Singletary had been the same man at home that he was in public. If the public Pastor Singletary had been the same as Daddy Singletary, I'm pretty sure that it would have broken the chains of the generational curse of our family. It breaks my heart that he was never able to see how his desire for reputation and approval, coupled with his refusal to confess his sin to God, ruined him and most of his children.

Sadly, all the energy he spent projecting one character in public, while living another at home, finally wore him down. He left his family and his public display of faith in God. His double life finally got the better of him.

But I don't have to tell you all of this. If you haven't been personally upended by the wake of someone who possessed a hidden bad character, you've surely read about it or seen it on the news. High-profile athletes and entertainers, who were at one time role models, eventually break down under the pressure of their fame and image. Or the pastor, who was adored by his congregation for his eloquent and moving sermons, falls prey to sexual impurity, financial misdeeds, or a number of other things.

It can be a long and painful fall from the perches we put ourselves on when we choose to become our own press agents and publicists in an effort to make ourselves look better than we really are. That is, without a doubt, the most dangerous game we can play.

But character formed on the inside will stand the test. It's unassailable, and it's durable. Even when everything seems to be lined up against us, if we have been shaped and molded in our inner being by God, we can't be destroyed. We are indestructible.

Either way, our true character can't be hidden for long. For better or worse, who we are on the inside will be exposed for everyone to see.

2. CHARACTER IS NOT ABOUT REPUTATION BUT LIFESTYLE

I had to learn this lesson the hard way.

VISUALIZE YOUR GREATNESS

Several years ago, as I was developing my skills and reputation as a public speaker, I was invited to speak to a large group of people about what it means to be truly successful. I really thought that I did a fantastic job of talking to them about living our best lives and treating people with humility, generosity, and respect.

As soon as I finished speaking, people flocked to me and told me how my speech was life-changing for them, and that they would immediately implement what I had shared.

Honestly? I was on cloud nine. I felt great about what I had done. I stood a little taller, and my chest puffed out a little further.

I'm kind of ashamed of myself now because as soon as the approval started flowing my way, I violated my own words. I remember thinking, *I'm getting pretty good at this public speaking thing. I'm really helping people live better lives, really making a difference in the world.*

Once the event ended, I hurried to my car, anxious to get back home to Kim and the kids. I hadn't gone far before I realized that my gas tank was close to empty, so I pulled into the first station I came to. I drove slowly up to the pump, got out, and swiped my credit card.

"Unable to process payment!"

I tried it again. Same message on the screen. So, I tried it once more with the same results.

I'll admit that I was a little frustrated when I walked up to the cashier.

"Hey, something is wrong with the card reader on that pump!"

The young man was maybe seventeen or eighteen years old, and he happened to be a Bears fan.

"Dude! You're Samurai Mike, Mike Singletary, aren't you?" He began to reenact the Super Bowl Shuffle like I hadn't seen it before. Unfortunately, I was a little short with him. "Look, I need to get on the road. Can we just get that pump working so I can get home?"

PRINCIPLE 5: CHARACTER

He pushed a few buttons and told me it was ready, but when I tried to run my card again, I got the same results. By this time, I was really frustrated. Truthfully, I was getting a little angry.

The young man apologized and said, "I don't understand it! Why don't you try another pump? By the way, Mr. Singletary, can I have your autograph?"

I told him that I would give it to him after I had pumped my gas, gone back to my car, and moved it to another pump. Would you believe it? Same results.

By this time, my anger was really getting the better of me. I stomped back into the store, walked up to the counter, and said (with more than a little aggression in both my voice and posture), "What kind of place are you guys running here? Can I get gas or not? All I want to do is fill up and go home!"

I could see the fear in the young man's eyes. "Maybe you should pay with cash," he stammered. The problem was that I had very little cash on me, but I gave him what I had and went back to put a few gallons in the tank.

As I was replacing the nozzle in the pump, I glanced back at the young man staring at me from behind the counter. I could still see the fear in his eyes. But it was the disappointment I saw that cut me like a knife. Until then, I had been his role model. I could clearly see that I had blown it with him.

With my ego wounded by my own arrogance, I shuffled back into the store with my tail between my legs. To be honest, I was ashamed of myself.

"Son, you still want that autograph?"

I fully expected him to say yes, but he didn't. "No thanks," he mumbled. When I insisted, "It's no problem," he turned his head the other way and whispered, "It's OK ... I'm good."

I don't know if you've ever had one of those moments when you did something so stupid or outrageous that you couldn't stop thinking about it for hours or even days afterward. That was me that day. All the way home, God really let me have it about how I had allowed myself to get all bloated about the reputation I was building as a public speaker, and yet I hadn't paid attention to the needs of that young gas station attendant.

God reminded me of my public words about treating others with humility, generosity, and respect. And every time he used one of my own words against my spirit, it was like another slap in the face. Years before, I had crucified (with Christ) the old Mike Singletary with his outbursts of anger, but on that day, the old Mike was trying to crawl out of his grave and resurrect himself. Every time I think he's dead, he shows himself in other ways.

If I had one redeeming moment in response to that ugly display of my old spirit, it was that I humbled myself *before God* once again, renewed my commitment *to him*, and resubmitted myself *to him* to be shaped and molded *by him* into the image of Christ.

I should have remembered that my character isn't what I put on display before a crowd of people who don't really know me; it is the life I live when no one is there to give me approval. On that sad day, my character had been revealed in the way I treated that young man, and I didn't like what I saw.

3. WHEN YOU RECOGNIZE GOOD CHARACTER, CHASE IT DOWN!

This section is a lot like the one from principle 2 about the importance of being conscious of the company we keep, except it goes a step further. I've already told you about the group of guys that I hung out with in middle school. With my mother's encouragement, I stopped

PRINCIPLE 5: CHARACTER

long enough to observe their behavior, projected where they were going to wind up, and decided we had very different ideas about our futures. What they wanted and chased would not lead me to a place where my vision would be realized. So, I ran from them, not because I was afraid of them, but because I was fearful of where they would lead me.

I stopped running from my fears and began running toward my vision.

Many years ago, when I was with the Bears, I began to seek out people who would challenge me to aim higher and allow my faith in God to touch all areas of my life—my marriage, my role as a father, and my job. I wanted God to have it all, so I made myself available to a group of men who wanted the same thing. We all committed ourselves to being mentored by one another, holding one another accountable, and to encouraging one another.

Sometimes, our time together could be comforting and soothing, but it could also be brutal in its honesty. We didn't hold back.

Our local chaplain led the group, but one week, he was unable to attend, so a guest pastor stepped in. I was blown away by the way he seemed to have such a firm grip on what it takes to be a man of God. I thought he was speaking directly to me.

When the formal accountability session ended, we all gathered for refreshments and fellowship. But I could hardly enjoy myself because I was thinking about the power of the visiting preacher's words. Without even knowing me, his presence had cut me like a knife as I'd realized that I still had so far to go in my walk as a man of God.

But his words also gave me a confident hope that I could be a better husband, father, church member, and citizen than I had been up to that point. It was true that I was living a pretty good life at the

VISUALIZE YOUR GREATNESS

time, but I'd listened to no more than a few words from this man's mouth when I realized that I didn't want to settle for "pretty good."

After a few minutes of fellowship time, I turned and noticed that the visiting pastor was sliding out the door, so I quickly followed and caught up with him in the parking lot.

"Pastor, could I have a minute of your time?" I asked him. "I want to ask a favor of you. I heard what you said about what a godly man looks like, and I would like to ask you if you would mentor me in all those areas of my life that I feel need to improve. I want to be a better husband and father. I want to grow in my faith in the Father. Would you do that?"

I'll admit that it was a bold move to approach a man I barely knew and ask so much of him, but I can tell you one thing—I was glad that he agreed to do it.

This was another of those pivotal relationships in my life. Over time, he encouraged me and built me up, but he was also willing to tell me what I did not want to hear. He wasn't impressed one single bit that I was Mike Singletary, All-Pro linebacker for the Chicago Bears. I suppose he was so comfortable in his own skin because he was such good friends with God. When a man knows God, who am I by comparison?

Living a life centered on the goodness of God does not come naturally. It's always a good idea to find someone who is both pursuing that life and has had some measure of success at living it out every day. I don't know for certain that God sent him my way, but you couldn't convince me otherwise. I saw him as a godsend. So, when he did visit our group, and I saw his character, I latched on to him with a firm grip. I soaked up what he said, but I also soaked up how he lived. I tried to imitate him as he imitated Christ.

As it turns out, that was one of the best moves of my life.

4. YOU CAN'T CASH A CHARACTER CHECK AT THE BANK

"You gotta do what you gotta do!"

That's just street language for "by hook or by crook!" What we really mean when we say that is, "Whatever we have to do to get ahead is all OK. Even if someone else is wounded in the process of scratching and crawling over the backs of others on the way to the top, it's all right because the outcome is what really matters."

The problem with that strategy is that any success we enjoy when we rise to the top that way is always going to be short lived. Any money we make is going to burn a giant hole in our pockets, and it won't be long before we dig in to find only a few bucks and realize that we have squandered it all. Trust me! I've seen more than my fair share of celebrity athletes, who were paid millions of dollars to play a game, wind up in bankruptcy court not too many years later. Chances are, so have you.

Or how about the men and women we've all known who "steal" another person's spouse because they thought he or she was their soulmate, only to have the sweetness of their "love" turn sour in their mouths not long afterward?

We may be able to put the check in the bank or the woman in our bed, but good character isn't cashed that way. If someone really desires something that lasts, they should say, "I gotta do what is right," rather than "I gotta do what I gotta do." This kind of commitment builds character that lasts for a lifetime, and it always winds up satisfying us in ways that a self-centered approach never can.

But there is another benefit, one which can't be overstated, of doing what is right, and it has to do with how we process our own mistakes. If I'm self-centered in my approach to life, I have no way to handle my own blunders properly and safely. When it's all about

VISUALIZE YOUR GREATNESS

me and my outward "character," rather than what is inside of me, it's easy to wind up wallowing in self-pity and self-doubt because we have no way to deal with our sin. After a while, the load becomes too heavy to carry.

True character, especially that which is driven by an unshakable faith in God, allows us to admit, without shame and overpowering guilt, that we are imperfect, and that we are going to make mistakes and even sin. The reason that we can admit this so freely is that our hope isn't in ourselves but in God's grace. Our hope is in the love of God, not in our love for self. And when we are assured of God's love for us, we can confidently know that nothing—no mistake or misdeed—is greater than his affection for us.

There is no safer place for you and me to be. If his love is a check, it's one we can cash right here and now. Money in the bank. But the good news is that it's not a one-and-done deal. It's like the movie *Groundhog Day*, where the main character wakes up every day, only to find out it's a repeat of the day before. In God's version of that movie, we wake up every day with a new check we can cash, and with it comes new opportunities to submit to God's work in our spirits and in our character.

True character relies on this promise: We get the chance to learn from our mistakes and build on our successes.

5. THE MORE WE SEEK GOOD CHARACTER, THE MORE IT GROWS

My brother Charlie? A lot of people just called him Sonny Boy! And truth be told, he was my mom's favorite. But Sonny Boy always had an excuse.

"Why am I the only one who can't make it? Is it because I'm too dark-skinned?"

PRINCIPLE 5: CHARACTER

This may come as a shock to many non-Black people, but in the African American community, you can be considered either too dark or too light. Charlie was so dark-skinned that some of the residents of Sunnyside gave him a nickname that many now consider racist—they called him "Black Sambo."

My sister Rudell also had a dark complexion, and the kids taunted her with chants of "Black Rudy! Black Rudy!" I clearly recall her hiding in her bedroom and weeping because of the teasing she received.

They were actually two of the best-looking people I knew. But the problem was that some other Black people wouldn't let them forget their skin tone. "You're too dark, so you must not be that smart."

On the other hand, if you were too light skinned, you must really think you're somebody special. Kids with lighter complexions caught hell, too.

You can't win for losing with some folks. I don't know why some people in Sunnyside put such emphasis on skin tone. Maybe it was the fruit of living in a culture where basic human rights were given to people with white skin but denied to darker people. I think it was a way of saying, "I may be Black, but I'm not as Black as you!"

Whatever the reason, it was painful for those who were victimized by it. And it certainly took a toll on Charlie. His skin tone was darker than that of both of our parents. In fact, his complexion was really quite dark. For him, being darker was like a large millstone tied around his neck. He couldn't get past it. His skin tormented him so much that he would sometimes pour bleach into his bathwater and bathe in it to try and make himself lighter. All because the taunts distorted his view of his looks and who he was.

But I saw Charlie as tall, dark, and handsome, and a lot of girls thought so as well. As a matter of fact, I admired him. Unfortunately, my father was so young and immature when Charlie was born, he was not equipped to embrace a son who was darker than both him and my mom. My dad brought a lot of baggage from his upbringing and his broken relationship with his own father, and he projected all of that onto Charlie, his oldest son.

My mom constantly ran interference between my dad and Charlie. My dad was attempting to make Charlie a man, and my mom continued to feel guilty for not being able to protect him more. This pattern continued all of Charlie's life, which made it difficult for him to ever become all that God had created him to be. This beautiful Black man never realized how truly special he really was.

My next oldest brother, Charles, also had dark skin. Everyone in our community had more than one nickname. I always thought it was a Black thing, but I found out that rural Whites do it too. One of the names that Charles was given was "Pharaoh" because he was so mean.

He later changed his name to Jerome, maybe as a way to separate himself from our father.

Charles presented alternating personalities. One moment he was the nicest guy on the planet. He tended to his pigeons and bees, talking to them like they were his children. He planted and cultivated flowers and plants, which he used to make our property look more beautiful. Charles was the one who kept everything looking good around the house. He was also an incredible chef. In fact, he was the only person I knew who was a better cook than my mom.

He was all of that sometimes, a sensitive and kind man. The problem with Charles was that he could erupt in fits of anger at a moment's notice. Kind Charles would suddenly explode and become cruel and almost demonic.

I never knew why until I was almost grown.

In my junior year of high school, I came home from a track meet one day and curled up in my bed for a short nap. A few minutes later,

PRINCIPLE 5: CHARACTER

Charles stomped through the door and demanded of our mother, "Where's Mike?" When she told him, he burst into my room, jerked the covers off me, and said, "Get your ass out of that bed."

I was already in a horrible mood, so I told Charles, "I'm tired. I think you might want to leave me alone." But he didn't let up. He ordered me out of bed again and complained about Mom letting me lie around and stay in bed all day.

By this time, momentum was beginning to build for me at school. For one thing, my grades were beginning to reflect the hard work I was putting in. Not only that, but I had also received several letters from small colleges that were interested in me playing football for their school. Even my coaches were starting to notice how much I had improved and were saying things like, "Singletary, it looks like you're gonna get a scholarship soon from a Division I school."

Needless to say, I was beginning to feel that I had physically become a man. So, I bolted out of bed, bowed my chest at him, gritted my teeth, and let him have it. "If you say one more thing tonight, I'm gonna hurt you."

He was stunned! No one had ever heard me talk like that before. I wasn't one to get involved in fights and brawls. I never ran my mouth at anyone. So, when I laid down the law with Charles, he knew that he was only a few seconds away from biting off more than he could chew.

I will never forget his response. Tears formed in the corners of his dark eyes, and he began to sob. I had never heard him weep like that. I did remember my mother crying when my dad left her high and dry, but her tears weren't so much for herself as they were for her kids. Her weeping was born out of her lament, a plea for God to intervene and for God to provide for her children.

VISUALIZE YOUR GREATNESS

This was different. The tears running down my brother's face were those of his own moral and spiritual collapse. Charles was caught up in a web of deceit, a tangle of lies. The problem was that I had no idea.

He told me about the day that our father had left one of his male relatives in charge of me and my other siblings while he went to pick up my mom. It was while this man was supposed to be watching the rest of us that he took advantage of Charles's youth and naivety.

"Man, he raped me! I was just a young kid, and he raped me!"

I didn't know exactly how to respond, other than to tell him the only thing I knew to be true. "I love you, Charles. You are my brother, and nothing is going to change that. I am proud of you, and I will fight for you."

I wish that I had possessed the wisdom to tell Charles that events do not define us. Life happens to all of us. I wish that I could understand when things like that happen. But what happens to us along the way doesn't change the fact that God loves us and has a plan for each of our lives. Through our pain and setbacks, we just have to keep our eyes on God, forgive those who hurt us, and continue to take the high road.

And above all, I wish that Charles could have found out that nothing that had ever happened to him was a surprise to God. He would have found out that God's love for him was so complete that he could have obeyed God, no matter what he told him to do.

I didn't know it then because I was just a young man barely out of boyhood, but I know it now. Jesus himself had multiple encounters with people who had believed Satan's lies about sex. There was the woman at the well in John 4 who had five husbands to her credit and was shacking up with a guy who wasn't her husband at the time Jesus met her. And in John 8, Jesus met a woman who was caught in the

PRINCIPLE 5: CHARACTER

act of adultery and was dragged (probably half naked) through the streets of Jerusalem by a scheming mob of religious men.

We all have something that no one else knows about, something we wouldn't dare talk about. Just know one thing: There are no secrets with God, and he still loves us.

Most of the preachers and theologians didn't care about these women, but Jesus did. Those men had no compassion for the guilt and shame the women felt, but he did. Not once, not a single time, did Jesus ever speak to even the lowliest of sinners with anything that resembled condemnation and judgment.

What he did, instead, was to call them to himself. He even told the woman caught in the act in John 8, *"Is there no one left to condemn you? Then neither do I! Now, be on your way and stop believing in Satan's lies."*

There is something else that I think is worth mentioning too. While Jesus never verbally ripped sinners, he often spoke harshly to the Pharisees—the religious elite, who were the preachers and the theologians of his day. He told them that they were like "whitewashed tombs," a "brood of vipers," and like a dirty bowl that was clean on the outside but filthy on the inside.

Did he have it backward? Or do we? I think we know the answer to that question. People who live with addiction to the seedier kinds of sin already feel condemned. Why would we need to point out their weakness to them again? Charles already felt condemned, even though he had done nothing wrong. Because I knew that, I chose instead to remind him of my love for him, and more importantly, of God's love for him.

Why would anyone who professes love for God want to pile on a man who was bullied and teased his whole life and was raped as a young boy? Shouldn't God's people desire to respond to these divine

VISUALIZE YOUR GREATNESS

encounters with our fellow sinners with the same kind of compassion as Jesus did? Shouldn't we desire to invite them to attend the same party in the throne room of God that we enjoy every day?

We don't modify our behavior in order to enjoy God, but we learn to enjoy God and allow him to transform us, to mold and shape us into the image of his son. And even though we get this backward far too often, this is what God's Word says to do.

First and foremost, we have one responsibility as believers. And that is to love God with all our hearts, minds, souls, and strength, and to love our neighbors as ourselves. God says that when we seek him with all our hearts, we will find him. So, wherever you are, whoever you are, and whatever you've done, and whatever has happened to you, just remember this: Events don't determine who we are. God's Word does. God is the only one who has the authority to give us identity because he is our maker.

Bottom line? God is asking us to trust him. When we trust him, we read his Word and seek to obey it.

Unfortunately, after Satan had driven the final nail in Charles's "coffin" when he was sexually abused, Charles was so uncomfortable with his own skin, and so unable to trust God, that he also bathed with bleach in an attempt to erase the stain of that horrible event.

Charles overturned every rock in his life looking for that one thing that would make him feel better about himself. What he was really looking for was that one thing that would explain his life. I have often wished that I could have encouraged him more often to look under the Jesus rock because it was the only place where he could have found the love that he so desperately longed for.

In some respects, I was a lot like Charles. I was quiet, and I didn't like to fight unless I was backed into a corner. And as I've said, I was kind of a mama's boy. The difference between Charles and me was

PRINCIPLE 5: CHARACTER

that I had never experienced the kind of abuse that he had endured. But I came close one time.

When I was about ten years old, my father began taking me to my uncle's house so I could stay with his stepdaughter and older stepson while the two of them went out partying.

I didn't mind because the girl was cute, and I was just beginning to think about how awesome girls were.

Her brother, who was supposed to be watching out for us, kept asking me if I liked him better than his sister. At first, I thought it was a joke. At least, I did until he took me into his bedroom and tried to touch me in a way that I knew was wrong.

He moved toward me, but before he could touch me, the phone rang. His sister answered the call, looked at me, and said, "It's your mama, Mike!" I took the receiver from her hand and heard my mother say in the sternest voice possible, "Get out of that house right now and start walking home. I mean right now!"

Coincidence? Luck? A close call? You can think that if you want to, but I'm not buying it. I was seconds away from having the same detrimental life-changing experience as Charles. I didn't waste one more second in that house. Without even saying goodbye, I bolted out of the door and walked the five miles home as fast as my little legs could carry me.

My mom had no way of knowing what was about to happen, but something or someone spoke to her and warned her to act quickly to keep me from harm's way. I believe that was God.

I'll say more about my other brothers later, but I'll tell you this now—they all had more talent and innate ability than I ever did. However, they wasted their lives because of the things they believed. And because of what they believed, they refused to do what they should have done. I believe they all heard the same voice from God

VISUALIZE YOUR GREATNESS

that I heard, but fear, guilt, hate and shame overwhelmed them and prevented them from really hearing.

Why didn't they pursue character in the same way I did? I don't fully know the answer to that question. Maybe it's because my mother continually pointed me toward a bright, infinite future with God. Or maybe it's because I was the baby.

Once my dad left, she had more time to devote to me. In addition, he wasn't there to undo everything she tried to do, like he had done with my siblings. Mom had my undivided attention. We spent hours together several times a week from the time I was twelve years old until I left for college. She explained life to me as she shared Bible verses and real-life experiences. She could identify ways in which I was like my father, and she worked to shape and mold those qualities so that they could be used for good.

I just wish my siblings had been able to hear my mom's voice uninterrupted by my dad's. My siblings had it rough. Just like in many other families, there were so many mixed messages coming at them that it was hard for them to get it. Our home life made it difficult for them to see a loving God.

I loved every one of them with my whole heart. Mom did a great job of trying to lead us spiritually, and I now believe that my dad meant well, but I wish that he had been the one to set the tone in our family. Unfortunately for him and the rest of us, however, he was an example of how unforgiveness can kill a family. I believe that all of us, especially my siblings, would have been better for it if he had learned to forgive his own father, who put him out at the age of thirteen.

I'm just thankful that I heard what my mom said about character. As the years went on, I noticed that what she had told me was true— the more I pursued character, the more of it I had. My character wasn't perfect then. In fact, it's not perfect now. But those early baby steps

PRINCIPLE 5: CHARACTER

of faith and the pursuit of character gave me a path to travel that led me to God's version of the good life. I haven't "arrived" yet, but I am continuing to be shaped and molded by God from the inside out. My heart is to make a tremendous difference in my generation.

So, here's where the rubber meets the road. What was the difference between me and my brothers Charlie and Charles? We had the same parents and grew up in the same neighborhood. Why me and not them? How come they lived such broken lives characterized by fractured relationships and addictions while I did not?

Well, first, I wasn't better than they were. My siblings were, in many respects, smart, talented, handsome, and beautiful. They were good people.

But by the time my father's negative influence was purged from our house, the damage had already been done as far as they were concerned. When he left, I was just coming of age and formulating my own identity. This is the difference between us; the noise was eliminated, and I was able to hear God's voice more clearly. And when I heard it, I sought out the character of Christ. I tried to imitate him as well as my mom, who was following and worshipping him.

But here's what I wish that I could tell them—it's not too late to pursue good character. I still must be reminded of this because my own character isn't fully grown yet. And while it's true that I might not be able to undo some of the collateral damage of my mistakes (as in the case of the young man at the gas station), we are always better off seeking and nurturing good character.

6. WE MUST TRAIN OUR CHARACTER IN PRIVATE TO DISPLAY IT IN PUBLIC

I've already mentioned Coach Oliver Brown, my defensive coordinator and track coach at Worthing High School. If I had only two words

VISUALIZE YOUR GREATNESS

to describe him, they would be *uncompromising* and *uncensored*. He never minced words when it came to inspiring me and my teammates to strive for excellence.

The one thing I learned from him that I've never forgotten is his belief that champions are made from blood, sweat, and hard work. That's why his practices were so brutal. Coach always carried a stopwatch and a whistle that he swung around on his finger. We knew that the more he swung that whistle, the more intense the workouts were about to become.

I never ran the 440 competitively, but I did run it in practice. If you've never run track, you need to know that it's at about the 330-yard mark that your knees begin to buckle, and your lungs expand so much that you feel as if they are about to burst. You want to give up a hundred yards before the finish line. We called it "having the monkey on your back."

Coach Brown knew all about the temptation to stop before we finished, so he would yell out, "Go! Don't stop! Push yourself! Let's go!" He pushed us hard to find out who we were inside because of his conviction that championships were won before we ever hit the track or the football field on Friday night. It's an inside job.

He also taught me to go home after practice and visualize running into that wall that tempted me to give up, and then visualize him screaming out, "Push! Go! Don't stop! Turn on the afterburners!"

As I said, I wasn't a quarter-miler, but I practiced this strategy in preparation for what I did compete in—the shot put. I went home and visualized combining my technique, speed, and power to perfection. As a result, I was almost flawless in the meets.

This came in handy when I got to Baylor University. One of my coaches was a Dr. Jekyll and Mr. Hyde character named Corky Nelson. Off the field, he was kind and funny. But, man, when practice

PRINCIPLE 5: CHARACTER

began, he became another person altogether. I actually thought he was wicked, always riding my tail even when I was doing exactly what he had told me to do. Over and over, he screamed at me in his thick Texas accent, "Sangletary," (that's what it sounded like), "you're gonna do it perfectly—my way—every time. I saw your goals that Coach had you write out. Do you even know what all-American means? We're about to find out what you've got!"

Then he would turn up the heat on me a few notches.

It's still emotional for me to recall how, after practice, I would retreat into my dorm room and gaze in the direction of Houston, overcome with a desire to just quit and go home. But as bad as I desired to run back to my mother and the familiarity of the easy life, becoming Mama's baby boy all over again, I didn't quit.

Instead, I looked at myself in the mirror and repeated what I'd been telling myself all along: "I *am* going to be an all-American. I'm going to be great! I'm going to be the best! I don't know how, and I don't know when, but come hell or high water, by God's grace, I'm doing it." It was there in my dorm room that I had conversations with God about living up to the dream he had given me.

One day, Coach Nelson ordered me to follow him to the bleachers high up in the stadium after practice, and he challenged me. "Sangletary, you want to be an all-American. Is that right?"

Tears began to form in my eyes and trickle down my cheeks as I answered him. "Yes, sir!"

He looked directly at me and laid down the gauntlet. "Well, I'll tell you how to be noticed. When we play Alabama this week, you'll be facing one of the best centers I've ever seen. He's good! Really good! He's a two-time all-American by the name of Dwight Stephenson. Quick and big and strong. If you can get twenty tackles on him this Saturday, that'll get you noticed."

123

VISUALIZE YOUR GREATNESS

After the game was over, I had twenty-seven tackles to my credit. While I was still standing on the field, an older man came up to me wearing a houndstooth hat and said, "Son, you're the best linebacker I've seen since Lee Roy Jordan." When he walked away, Coach Nelson said, "Do you know who that was? That was Coach Bear Bryant."

Finally, I was beginning to reap the rewards of hard work. People were beginning to notice me. After all, when the great Bear Bryant takes note of you, that's a big deal, right?

But that's just football. I've often wondered how my life would have turned out if I had been satisfied with that, just excellence in football. I don't think it would have been a pretty picture because everything good in my life—Kim and the kids, the godly men who speak truth to the lies in my life, even the opportunities I get to speak to groups across the country—would have never happened.

I'm not overstating it—my persistent hounding of God to change me, to use me and develop me as a man, and to shape and mold my character is the foundation of every single good thing I've enjoyed.

Let me give you an example of what I'm talking about.

Early on, I imagined scenarios where I was confronted with one of those triggers that caused me to lose my temper. In my mind, I would visualize someone calling me a name, even the N-word, and I would practice responding appropriately. I would ask myself questions like, *Do I fight? Do I go to jail over this? Am I willing to get injured? Am I willing to destroy my reputation?*

I even imagined the worst-case scenario: What if they said something about my Mama? My first response was, "Well, we may have to fight about that. It's a Black thing." All joking aside, whatever we want to see in our lives, we must visualize first. As I said, it's an inside job.

124

PRINCIPLE 5: CHARACTER

The good news is that once we begin to give God access to our hearts and minds, we eliminate the fear that someone is going to discover who we really are because we aren't trying to hide anything anymore. We become open books that anyone can read.

This is the foundation of liberation. The growing development of a godly inner character is what slays guilt and shame. Think about it; why would I be concerned with what other people think about me if I know that God's Spirit is living in me? If I have God's approval and know that he's working on me from the inside out, what else do I need?

7. WE CAN BUILD CHARACTER EVEN WHEN WE ARE FACING FEAR, DOUBT, AND NAYSAYERS

Hey, everyone wants a trophy. I get it. But not everyone gets one after every game. In fact, there is often a long pause between the times we receive recognition for the good things we do.

Life can be brutal. If anyone understands that, I do. But I'll let you in on my secret sauce, a principle that keeps me pursuing the inner growth of my character, even when the world is throwing all kinds of junk my way. The following is something I've lived by for a long time:

> *When the quest for greatness gets really tough, who will still be there once the dust settles? Who will say, "I'll be back tomorrow, even if no one else shows up? I'm here until we cross the finish line!"*

When it comes to building character, this is the bottom line. It is in the commitment to stay until the job is done, whatever that job is. Character isn't about trophies, not even a little bit.

But for all of us, life really does throw thousands of obstacles in our way, each with the potential to derail our commitment to

VISUALIZE YOUR GREATNESS

finishing what we started. And when we are enduring attacks from outside of ourselves, and no one notices or tells us that we're doing a good job, it can be hard to keep on pushing to the finish line.

One of those obstacles happened to me on June 4, 2004. I had not been coaching with the Ravens for very long when that day rolled around. As I was wrapping up a meeting, I received a phone call from my sister Linda that would rock my world.

"Mike, Mom fell and she's not moving. I called the paramedics, but I'm really afraid, Mike!"

I'm not going to lie. This sucked the air out of my lungs. Mom had put up with so much in her eighty-two years. Besides my dad's abuse, some of my siblings tormented her to death by their failure to launch. She loved all ten of us with an unwavering affection. She believed in all of us, seeing unlimited potential in every single one of her kids. So, the fact that many of them had squandered that, for whatever reason, was a heavy burden for her. She knew the damage my father had done to them, and she felt guilty for not putting a stop to it, even though I don't think she really had the power to do that.

By the time Linda called me, I had been aware of Mom's declining health for a while. So, I had been praying for four or five years for God to give me a little more time with her, for him to extend her life just a bit.

I tried to be strong for Linda. "She's going to be OK, Linda! I'm going to pray and call you right back."

I went to a quiet place and began to bang on heaven's door. "Lord, let me see her one more time. Don't let her go like this!" What I meant was that I wanted God to let her get up off the floor and be OK again.

But I heard a voice in my head that asked, "Are you sure you want to see her one more time?"

"Yes, Lord, I am."

The voice said, "Look up!"

I did what he commanded me, and it was like a movie. I saw my mother. I saw her friends who had gone on before her. I saw my grandmother. And Mom was jumping from one cloud to the next, giggling and squealing like a little girl. She appeared to be about twelve years old, and she was having the time of her life.

I pondered what I was seeing for a second or two, and then I told God, "No, Lord … do not bring her back." From that moment on, I was good with what I had seen and was overjoyed that Mama was experiencing a joy she had never known while she was on earth.

If you had asked me five minutes before Linda called if I was ready to lose my mom, I would have told you, "Absolutely not!" Besides Kim, Mom was my closest ally on earth. We didn't have much growing up, but she gave me everything she had. And no one besides Kim has ever loved me as much as my mother did.

It was the kind of news that could have destroyed me, if not for one thing. God had been training me and working on my character for years so that I would learn to trust him. And I'm not going to lie—until I saw the vision (or the dream or whatever you want to call it) of my mom enjoying the fruit of her faith, I couldn't imagine my life without her.

But once God opened my eyes to a reality I couldn't have seen otherwise, my grief was transformed into joy. My fleshly spirit was tempted to believe what Satan was telling me: "Your mom is dead! This is the end of her! Be afraid!" But what God showed me gave me the power to call Satan a liar.

If I was going to correctly understand the death of a godly woman such as my mom, God would have to teach me. And what he showed me was that death for those who love God is not final. I found out

VISUALIZE YOUR GREATNESS

that Mom was more alive than ever—she had simply been transported, promoted out of this world into the presence of the eternal God.

I don't know whether I would have seen this if God had not been chipping away at my character to increasingly shape me into the image of his Son. What I do know is that being led by God allowed me to see my mom's death for what it was.

You won't believe what happened once I saw my mom in the clouds. Out of my fear and doubt, and despite Satan tempting me with the thought that this was the end for Mama, I never shed another tear. That's right! I didn't really cry anymore after that. For the first time, I was able to see Mom with God and know that he had already told her, "Well done, my good and faithful servant."

If you think that's strange, I would say that weeping for a woman who was enjoying her new life in ways that she never had before would have been the stranger response. My eyes weren't dry because I didn't love my mom; they were dry because I did love her. I was so happy for her that I couldn't mourn or weep. Why would I grieve a woman's death when she was now experiencing an ecstatic and exuberant life such as the one I had envisioned?

When I saw what God showed me, it set my inner character ablaze. I grew by leaps and bounds, not in spite of the circumstances of my mom's collapse and death, but because of them. What could have derailed an ungodly man's life turned out to be something that worked for my own good.

This is, by the way, exactly what the Bible says: *"And we know that in all things God works for the good of those who love him, who have been called according to his purpose." (Rom. 8:28 NIV)*

Notice that it doesn't say that everything works out like we want it to, rather that everything eventually works out for our good. That's not the same thing. I didn't see the truth of this when Linda first called me. But once I was permitted to see the hidden reality, it was one of the best days of my life. Mama was finally able to fully enjoy what she'd been preparing for her entire life.

But there's something else we should also notice about this promise. It is conditional. It only applies to those who love God. When God stood back and surveyed his creation, he said that it was "very good." He hadn't yet formed the first humans, but we can safely assume that he felt the same way about our ancestors, such that he looked at them and said that they were "very good."

I know that this is true because of verses from the Bible such as, *"For God so loved the world that he gave his one and only son that whoever believes in him will not die but have eternal life" (John 3:16)*. Even if you are in open rebellion to God and his will, he loves you. And contrary to what we tend to think, God even likes you.

But he also honors your autonomy. He's not going to force you to believe him or follow him. That's up to you. But before anyone decides that loving God isn't worth it, just be aware that the promise that all things will work for your good isn't an option for you until you do love him. Until you submit to him, you're on your own.

In one sense, my mom received the goal of her faith in God on the day she died. But she had been living an eternal kind of life for most of her life. She lived confidently expecting that God was both good and faithful. She lived this way, despite the hard circumstances she faced, because of her firm belief that God would turn bad into good. This was her character, and I pray that it is mine too.

You may not be there yet. But know this—even if you're that person who has made all the wrong choices up to this point, it's not too late. Even if your spouse has abandoned you, or you've lost your job, it's not too late. Even if you are stuck in the deadly cycle

VISUALIZE YOUR GREATNESS

of addiction to drugs, alcohol, sex, pornography, or laziness, he still loves you. It's still not too late.

None of that has any effect at all on God's love for you. He still loves you. He still wants to work in your life in a way that allows you to live with a character that is confident that all things will work out for your good.

The problem? Well, God isn't the problem. We are! The question for you is this—are you going to continue to travel the same familiar, well-worn path that you've always walked on? Or are you going to turn over control of your life to God and allow him to develop in you the character that empowers you to tell yourself, "I'll be back tomorrow, even if no one else shows up. I'm here until we cross the finish line!"

If this is what you dedicate yourself to, I can promise you one thing: You will look back a year from now and say to yourself, "That was the best decision I ever made."

Be confident of this, that he who has begun a good work in me will be faithful to complete it, until the day of Christ Jesus. (Phil. 1:6)

PRINCIPLE 6
COMPETE

What an amazing opportunity to really understand, the toughest competition I will ever face is the one looking at me in the mirror. Will I be all that God has called me to be, and go beyond the limits others have placed on me?

Will I nourish the gifts and talents in me? Or will I lust and envy someone else's tree?

And will I accept the pruning that feels like pain, but in due time will be my gain?

Be confident of this, that He who has begun a good work in me will be faithful to complete it, until the day of Christ Jesus. (Phil. 1:6)

1. COMPETE

The word *compete* often evokes images of sweaty athletes grunting and straining as they try to dominate and humiliate their opponents in the arena.

VISUALIZE YOUR GREATNESS

To be sure, that is one connotation of the word. But I want to move past that definition and talk about something bigger and better than domination and control of our opponents.

In one sense, what I'm talking about is the fight for our own survival. But it's even more than that. Good competition, the type that is healthy and life affirming, is the kind that an individual enters into in pursuit of an exuberant life, to live better than we ever thought possible.

Let's be honest here. We all have some version of the really good life tucked away in the back of our brains. It is true that this life may seem unattainable to many of us at the moment, but at least we all know what it would look like if it were possible.

The problem we have is that there is also another version of the good life in our heads. At least it can seem like the good life to us because it requires very little effort. It's the one that is satisfied with just sliding along, going with the flow, settling for less, and being content with just fitting in.

These two versions are in competition with one another, each trying to persuade us to choose it over the other. The question we all must answer is "Which one will we choose?"

I'll share with you a little later about the fight I've chosen, but what about you? Are there areas of your life where you are just coasting and taking what life gives you, even though you have some idea of what you wish your life could be like if only you knew how to live it? Are you striving for that better version, or are you settling for the few scraps that the rest of the world tosses your way? Or worse, have you just thrown in the towel and given up, allowing life to throw as many punches at you as it can without any resistance from you at all?

Look, I get it. We can feel trapped in our circumstances, thinking that we aren't all playing on a level field.

132

PRINCIPLE 6: COMPETE

Some enter the arena with a head start over others. They are the ones fortunate enough to be born into a community and family where success was a generational blessing. In my opinion, this is what families are supposed to do for their kids: Teach them what a good life looks like, and then give them the tools to live it. The Bible instructs parents to *"Train up a child in the way he should go; even when he is old, he will not depart from it" (Prov. 22:6).* If your mom and dad did this for you, you are blessed.

But there are others who were never taught to compete at all. In all probability, their parents didn't possess those skills either. Their communities and families experienced the opposite of generational blessing. They, along with their parents and grandparents, have never known what real greatness looks like. So, if we tell them that they should enter the race, they are likely to say, "Race? What race? I have no idea what you're talking about."

I get it! Truly, I do! But everyone is in the race, whether we know it or not. There are no exceptions! Either we choose not to enter the arena, or we sit in the stands as spectators to watch others compete, or we stand paralyzed with our feet in the starting blocks, refusing to launch. The fortunate ones, however, take the bull by the horns and get after it.

Regardless of how we respond to the competition, one fact remains: There is a race going on, and our names have all been entered on the roster to compete. How well we compete, or even whether we choose to participate, is up to us.

This brings up another important point. I'm in the race, but I'm not competing against you. Not really. The real competition is between those two versions of life that are in my head—between failure and greatness.

133

VISUALIZE YOUR GREATNESS

The reason it's important for me to see it this way is that if I am only competing against others, I will lose at some point. Someone better will come along and knock me off my pedestal.

For example, Bill Gates was the richest man in the world from 1995 until 2007, and then he was again from 2009 to 2018, after which he lost the title to Jeff Bezos, the founder of Amazon.

I don't know if this bothered Bill Gates, but if being number one on the billionaire list was important to him, he had to be very disappointed. As if to prove my point, Forbes publishes a list called The World's Real-Time Billionaires, which is regularly updated to tell us who's moved up or down the ranks.

As I'm writing this, Elon Musk is number one with an estimated net worth of $401 billion. In case you are wondering, Bill Gates is down to number sixteen with a net worth of only $106 billion. Poor fellow!

The kind of competition I'm talking about is much more personal than one between me and the next fellow. If I'm worried about my fellow man, then I have taken my eyes off the right path. I'll find myself blaming someone else for my failures. But whining about the people in my way is nothing more than an excuse for refusing to participate in the competition for the direction of my life in the first place. Sadly, by complaining instead of competing, I've predestined myself to a life of misery. It traps me in the endless cycle of blame and shame.

If you want to destroy your dreams of the good life, this is how you do it. Take your eyes off God, compare yourself to others, and blame them for your sadness. Waste your time complaining. That should take care of it.

It's called giving up!

But competition and striving for a healthy life combat this inner urge to surrender to forces too great for us to overcome. It is the fight

PRINCIPLE 6: COMPETE

to endure and persevere, even when the idea that God has a purpose for us seems like a foolish idea. It is the knowledge that the only way we can be disqualified is if we choose to leave the race or, worse, to not even walk up to the starting blocks in the first place.

Now would be a good time to stop what we are doing and ask ourselves a few questions.

Are you satisfied with where your life is headed? Are you prepared to stop and evaluate where you are in life? Are you willing to identify the lies you've believed about your worth and potential and then pray for the kind of honest self-reflection that will allow you to discover your true purpose and calling? Will you enter the arena by choice and search for the answer to the question of who you are and who you want to be?

If you find yourself in bed at night, unable to sleep because you are thinking, *There has to be more to life than this*, then these are some good questions. But the problem is that we can't really find the answers to these questions inside our own minds.

I can tell you this—I couldn't move on from my own acceptance of mediocrity and failure until I humbly approached God and pleaded with him, "What do you want from me? What is my destiny? What is the purpose you have for me?"

The reason that his version of my identity is more reliable than my own is that he is eternal. And since he is eternal, he is infinite in wisdom. He sees all of creation, including time, all at once. He doesn't need to wait to see what our future holds—he holds the future in his hands.

This is what I began to compete for—to trust God's version of my dignity, worth, and destiny more than I did my own. And once I entered this lifelong competition to understand and put his version of my identity into practice, I discovered the truth I mentioned earlier—

VISUALIZE YOUR GREATNESS

God did not call me to be better than anyone. He only called me to become the best version of who he created me to be.

And here's the crazy thing—the best version of me is the version that teaches me to follow Jesus as he shapes and molds me. It really isn't about me at all, other than my desire to submit to him. He is the one who changes me. I'm just following him with a desire to learn from him and somehow to become like him.

The problem is that this doesn't just happen. I must fight for it. I have to push back against the lies that would lead me to believe that I can find goodness somewhere else. But as long as we're being honest with one another, let's just admit that nothing we find in those other places will fulfill us. No drug! No amount of alcohol or money! No sexual partner! No material possession! No amount of plastic surgery! None of it will calm that inner fear that there has to be something better than the dreadful feeling we are wrestling with in the dead of night.

So, we compete for God's will! We compete to know him and experience his presence!

I'm hoping that you can see how this kind of competition is superior to the dog-eat-dog competition that is presently devouring our culture and that tells us to "get while the getting is good." That kind of wisdom tries to convince us that the only way up is to climb on the backs of others in our effort to reach the top. Or, if it doesn't do that, it throws a wet blanket on the fire of our competitive spirit by telling us, "You aren't good enough! They'll say you're delusional if you try that! The risks and costs are too high! Don't do it!"

But we also need to be clear about the identity of our real opponent. We may be tempted to think that they are the person or the thought that is dragging us down. However, it's none of that. It's not your mom, who told you that you weren't pretty enough, or your

PRINCIPLE 6: COMPETE

dad, who constantly ridiculed your dreams and tried to tell you that you were a screwup.

The Bible says our struggle isn't really with other human beings at all. It's way bigger than that.

"For our struggle is not against flesh and blood, but against the rulers, against the authorities, against the powers of this dark world and against the spiritual forces of evil in the heavenly realms." (Eph. 6:12 NIV)

It's important for me to identify my real enemy to keep me from focusing on someone else, because focusing on "them" robs me of my power and will to fight. Worse than that, it keeps me from recognizing that a more powerful ally is with me in the ring, fighting hard for my prosperity.

He is the one in the arena with me who whispers, "You matter to me! You are anointed! You are chosen! You are one of a kind! I have a purpose for your life that will endure through the ages!"

So, the answer to the question "Who do you want to be?" boils down to this—which voice will we fight to hear? Which voice will we listen to?

I don't personally know you, but I know something that you and I have in common. At any point in our lives, both of these voices are talking to us.

One of them is like one of those robocallers trying to convince us to buy an expensive (and sometimes worthless) extended car warranty. But that voice doesn't care about us at all. All it wants is to destroy our humanity, to steal God's love from our hearts. It doesn't concern the voice at all if we are wrecked by listening to what it has to say. In fact, that's its goal.

But here's the thing—while you may think that you only hear the negative voice, you are actually simultaneously hearing God's voice

VISUALIZE YOUR GREATNESS

in the background too. No matter who you are, you've desired more at some point. You've longed for better.

But where do you think that inner longing for a better life comes from? Animals may feel the pangs of hunger or the bitterness of excessive cold or heat. And they certainly do whatever they can to find food and warmth. But, as far as we know, they do not dream of a better life. From what I can tell, Kim's puppy doesn't sit around contemplating building a bigger doghouse with more amenities. As long as we provide food, shelter, and love, she's good to go. That's more than enough for her.

But with us, it's different. Since we are created in God's image, we are able to dream of a better life. Even if we think it's impossible, we still long for it and are disappointed when we don't get it. It's important for us to realize that the desire for something better comes from God, who speaks into our imagination and feeds it, even when we don't even know him or love him.

If we are unfamiliar with God, however, we might misunderstand this inner desire. We may think we should be treated better, that life is unfair. But this is not the voice of God; it is the voice of entitlement.

While we may be right about injustices done to us or that someone shortchanged us in life, focusing on those things will not satisfy our desires. In fact, dwelling on that kind of thing is a surefire way to live a bitter and lonely life. If someone wants to be disappointed, there's no better way to do it than by concentrating on the things over which they have absolutely no control.

If this describes you, I would encourage you to just stop in your tracks! Find a quiet place where you can meditate and reflect. Then I would invite you to approach God and ask Him to give definition to your dreams and a vision for how you can actually live out those desires.

PRINCIPLE 6: COMPETE

But here's the deal—once he speaks (and he will answer our prayer), we must both listen to and answer the call. When we are invited by God to participate in his purpose for us, it begins with a clear answer: "Yes! Yes, I will compete for your purpose!"

When we do that, what once seemed impossible suddenly begins to seem not only possible for us but likely.

Are you ready to compete for that?

Before you say yes, I should warn you that not everything will fall into place overnight. In fact, the road to living out your vision will be filled with potholes and wrong turns along the way. Like I have done several times, you will stumble! You will fail at some point!

But as my mother said when she challenged me to embrace the greatness God had in store for me, "When you get punched in the gut, here's what you do—you dust yourself off, get back in the ring, and keep on swinging until you are the only one left."

Without this commitment to getting back in the ring after a loss and swinging until we are the only one left, competition can be devastating. But the person who keeps on competing? That's something else!

I think about this sometimes when I flick on the light switch in a darkened room at my house. The electric light bulb is something we take for granted. But the inventor of the first commercially available light bulb, Thomas Edison, failed in his first 2,774 attempts. Think about that—almost three thousand failures! Knocked down time and time again, he got up, dusted himself off, and got back into the ring until he was the last man standing. And he didn't even know Rudell Singletary.

It's true that he was competing against Nikola Tesla and George Westinghouse, but he was also competing against himself, against a spirit of surrender to failure. I wonder, with all those "failures" and with Tesla and Westinghouse breathing down his neck, if Edison ever entertained the thought that it might be time to pull up stakes and move on to greener pastures? I'm glad he didn't.

This kind of competition that keeps on plugging to subdue the natural world is what we were created for.

So God created man in his own image; he created him in the image of God; he created them male and female. God blessed them, and God said to them, "Be fruitful, multiply, fill the earth, and subdue it. Rule the fish of the sea, the birds of the sky, and every creature that crawls on the earth." (Gen. 1:27–28)

What this really means is that we are most like him when we restore order to the chaos by competing to either change our circumstances or to find a way to keep on fighting despite them. We bear fruit, multiply, and subdue the natural world around us, not in a way that abuses it, but in a way that makes it more productive—a way that makes it better. In other words, we are always competing for the better outcome in every circumstance.

And if we accept this as God's mandate for our lives, it is also true that we will never experience real fulfillment, satisfaction, or joy until we choose to compete. If we leave the fight, we lose our purpose.

2. COMPETE FOR YOUR IDENTITY

So far, we've been talking about competing in the arena of life. But when we think about how enormous the war for our vision is, it can seem overwhelming. It can appear to be too big for us. But the truth is that the big war is really just a series of individual, smaller skirmishes along the way. A bunch of little battles. We win the war by winning one dogfight at a time.

PRINCIPLE 6: COMPETE

If you want to think about this in terms of athletic competition, I can promise you something. Not one single time did my team win by simply suiting up and walking out on the turf.

Instead, every game we won was the result of every player on the team competing by fighting hard to do his job the way he had prepared to do it. And we did it one play at a time. Even if the media "experts" said we didn't have a chance, we still competed hard, play-by-play, because we knew we were prepared. Even if we were favored by fifty points, we still fought hard. If we did that, we won. If we didn't, chances are that we lost.

The Bible says *this "is why we never give up. Though our bodies are dying, our spirits are being renewed every day." (2 Cor. 4:16 NLT)*

When God's vision becomes our vision, we don't stop competing because we know that he's on our side. And since we know that he is on our side, no matter how weary we become in the middle of the battle, we can have confidence that we will awaken tomorrow with a renewed spirit.

This became so much clearer to me a few days after I arrived on Baylor University's campus to begin my freshman year. My head coach, Grant Teaff, assembled all the incoming freshman players in the locker room for a meeting. There we were, all gathered together, trying to act like we belonged.

I don't remember what I expected him to say, but what he did say had more to do with life than it did with football. He taught us that humanity consists of four components—physical, spiritual, mental, and social. As life begins to unfold, we must fight for balance between them because each aspect affects all the others.

However, he went on to explain that it is from the spiritual aspect of humanity that all the others flow because it instructs us about

141

VISUALIZE YOUR GREATNESS

how we even got here in the first place. He told us that there are only two choices—either an infinite, almighty, sovereign God created us and everything else in the universe, or this all just popped up out of nowhere and for no reason at all. He challenged us to consider the implications of the two possibilities—either God created us in his image, or we accidentally evolved over eons of time.

Coach Teaff then asked us to think about our views regarding what happens after we die. Do we just die along with our bodies, which are then planted in the dirt and become fertilizer, or do we live on after death? One explanation of our existence leaves us with no hope at all because, at the end of the day (according to this story), we weren't even supposed to be here in the first place. We are accidents!

The other view, he continued, is very hopeful because a loving, infinite God is in all the details of our creation and the intricate design of the universe. If he's real, and if we trust him, then we can also trust the blueprint he has given us for how to live a great life.

All these years later, I'm still thankful for Coach Teaff and how he made it so clear to me. Both points of view about how we got here have consequences. One leads to nothing! As Tolstoy wrote when he summarized the godless culture of Russia, "You are an accidentally united little lump of something."[3]

The other point of view leads to purpose and infinite meaning!

So, yes, we must compete in every battle if we want to be winners. But no battle is more consequential for us than the battle for who we are. The Evil One offers one identity. But if we boil down his version of how we got here (which, by the way, he knows is a lie), it says that you and I don't really matter—we are just carbon.

God, on the other hand, promises to tell us exactly who we are and why we are here. And what he says about us is that we are

---

3   Leo Tolstoy, *A Confession* (CreateSpace Independent Publishing Platform, 1882).

PRINCIPLE 6: COMPETE

uniquely, fearfully, and wonderfully made in his image. We are formed and shaped by God on purpose. And because he created us, we are beautiful to God. We actually matter to him.

But before we can choose which narrative we will listen to, there's something we need to know: We can't trust Satan any farther than we can throw him. He is the father of all lies. In fact, he invented lying.

God, on the other hand, never makes empty promises that don't materialize. In fact, no matter how many promises God has made, they are always "Yes" in Christ. He always tells the truth. He didn't just invent the truth—he is truth.

So, a healthy competitive identity boils down to this: Who are you going to trust? Who will you listen to? And if you choose God's story, how hard are you willing to compete to depend on what he has told you about yourself?

Not to be too repetitive, but everyone's already chosen one story over the other. Here's the thing, however—even if you've been listening to Satan's story about yourself your whole life, it's not too late to call him out as a liar and begin listening to what God says about you instead. In the Bible, this is called repentance, which is just a word that means that you have turned away from the wicked narrative about your relationship with God and started to listen to what your Creator says instead.

The question I have for you is this: Will you choose to compete? In every battle? And most importantly, will today be the day that you choose to fight in every battle? Not tomorrow or next week, but today?

I guess your answer to that is going to depend entirely on how tired you've become of fighting losing battles, expecting something good to just magically appear.

It's your choice. Yes, I'll compete, or no, I won't. Yes, I will begin to compete today, right now, or I'll do it later. I pray for you to choose well.

VISUALIZE YOUR GREATNESS

We will talk about mental health a little more later, but I want to mention this here.

I am well aware of how difficult it can be to look at all the junk in our lives—with all of our accumulated bad habits and practices and with all the outside forces that seem lined up against us—and still have hope. If we aren't careful, we might find ourselves in a downward spiral, emotionally and spiritually, thinking that it's all just too much.

Apparently, this spiral is something that more and more Americans are experiencing. Even young people are not immune to it. Between January 2016 and December 2022, the monthly antidepressant dispensing rate increased by 66.3 percent.[4]

I'm no expert on mental health, but even I can see that something is happening, and what I see isn't good. Why, of all people, are kids so depressed that they are increasingly prescribed these medications? After all, we tend to think that people in that age group are in the prime of life, right? But, evidently, many kids don't see it that way. What's different at this particular stage of American history that wasn't true in 2015 and before?

As I said, I'm no expert. But the numbers don't lie, and I can read the numbers.

One indicator might be the absence of fathers involved in children's lives. According to the Pew Research Center, America has the highest number of children living in homes without a father—three times higher than the world average.

---

4   Kao-Ping Chua et al., "Antidepressant Dispensing to US Adolescents and Young Adults: 2016-2022," https://www.ncbi.nlm.nih.gov/, February 26, 2024, https://pmc.ncbi.nlm.nih.gov/articles/PMC10904889/#:~:text=Between%20January%202016%20and%20December,%25%2C%20from%202575.9%20to%204284.8.

According to some studies, the impact of fatherlessness on children is profound. Here are a few of those findings[5]:

- A girl whose father leaves before she is five years old is eight times more likely to have an adolescent pregnancy than a girl whose father remains in her home.

- African American girls are 42 percent less likely to have sexual intercourse before age eighteen if their biological father is present at home.

- Children who live without their fathers are more likely to have decreased school performance.

- Of all high school dropouts, 71 percent come from fatherless homes.

- Children who live without their fathers are, on average, more likely to choose deviant peers, have trouble getting along with other children, be at higher risk for peer problems, and be more aggressive.

I don't know, but maybe the breakdown of the family might be a contributing factor to this mental health crisis among children and young adults.

But I think that the root of the problem is even worse than that. In fact, fractured families are just a symptom of that bigger problem.

---

5   Jane Anderson, "The Impact of Family Structure on the Health of Children: Effects of Divorce," U.S. National Library of Medicine, November 2014, https://pmc.ncbi. nlm.nih.gov/articles/PMC4240051/#:~:text=Girls%20whose%20fathers%20left%20 the,2003).

VISUALIZE YOUR GREATNESS

Gallup's research shows that, from 1944 to 2011, 90 percent of all Americans believed in God. But by 2023, that number had declined to 81 percent. The decline is even steeper among younger people.[6]

The reason this matters, in my opinion, is that when we untether ourselves from an infinite God, we become rudderless. We lose our moral compass. It might be easy to indoctrinate our kids into believing that God either isn't real or that he's irrelevant, but it comes with a hefty price tag. And the price tag is this: Kids aren't stupid. They know that if God isn't defining our lives, then we're on our own.

I think that this explains the chaos and confusion that has taken our culture by storm. Nothing matters! And in the case of declining fatherhood, if God the Father doesn't exist or doesn't matter, then what need do we have for any kind of father, even a heavenly one?

Without an infinite God, there's no way to know how we got here or even why we are here. If God's not real, we are just here because we're here.

Talk about bleak! No wonder kids are depressed. We've taught them that they are just left to themselves, drifting on a sea of human opinion, which, at the end of the day, means absolutely nothing. As the old people used to say, opinions are like elbows. Everybody's got one!

I'm not just making this up. According to an article published by the National Institutes of Health's Library of Medicine in 2021, religion makes a difference in people's lives. A big difference. People who have higher levels of religious convictions experience lower levels of depression. They also commit suicide less often. Religious people have lower substance abuse issues. They are less likely to experience symptoms of bipolar disorder and PTSD.

---

6   "How Many Americans Believe in God?," Gallup.com, June 24, 2024, https://news. gallup.com/poll/268205/americans-believe-god.aspx#:~:text=Line%20graph%20 showing%20trends%20in,they%20are%20convinced%20God%20exists.

PRINCIPLE 6: COMPETE

According to some studies, one in four Americans over the age of eighteen suffers from a diagnosable mental illness.[7] Think about that for a moment—one-fourth of all the adults you know are fighting a mental health battle. And that's just the ones who've been diagnosed.

The last thing I want to do is to stigmatize anyone who is caught up in this horrible mental health crisis. To be honest with you, considering my upbringing, I could have been a mental health statistic myself. If not for the grace of God, I would have been.

I believe that the only reason I'm not a statistic is because I had the good fortune to have adults in my life who pointed me in a different direction. They taught me to not only see God, but to pursue him and to meditate on him and his Word. They taught me to compete like a warrior for God's purpose for my life.

I didn't understand at first, but I was beginning to retrain my mind to think about what God wanted me to think about. Until then, I had been just going with the flow, soaking up the culture.

As we talked about when we discussed the RAS, the most amazing thing about our minds is that they are trainable. God created the brain with the ability to give us the information it thinks we want.

The unconscious parts of our brains are on autopilot. For example, we seldom think about breathing, even though we do it twelve to fifteen times every minute on average. This means that you and I inhale and exhale almost twenty thousand times per day. But we don't think about it, because our unconscious mind just tells our lungs to do their job.

Our subconscious is where every experience and thought is stored. I've already mentioned this before, but it is such a part of

---

7   "Mental Health Disorder Statistics," hopkinsmedicine.org, June 20, 2024, https:// www.hopkinsmedicine.org/health/wellness-and-prevention/mental-health-disorder-statistics#:~:text=An%20estimated%2026%25%20of%20Americans,disorder%20 in%20a%20given%20year.

VISUALIZE YOUR GREATNESS

how we think and act that I'm going to say it again. It records, filters, and stores what we feed it, and then it tells us what it thinks we want to hear.

The funny thing about our subconscious is that it picks up every morning right where it left off the night before. This means that if we don't begin each day by taking control and intentionally changing what we feed our minds, one bad day rolls into one bad week, which rolls into one bad year after another.

So, this is how we compete for our mental health. We must change what we feed our minds. If the adage "garbage in, garbage out" is true, then it's also true that we can change the outcome of our lives by what we feed our minds. We can choose to meditate on the thought that God knows us, loves us, and has a purpose for us. This is far different from the bleak assessment of life that has taken so many of our fellow Americans prisoner.

The question for all of us is, "Will we compete for our mental health?"

When I was a young boy, I imagined that I had superpowers. I don't mean that I pretended to possess them, but I actually thought that I had them.

It's always kind of cute when a little kid thinks they are like Superman, but there comes a time when it stops being cute and becomes bizarre. So, when I became a man, I put away childish things.

The truth is that no one has superpowers. But we do have something in our arsenal that is even better than that. More than once, God's Word makes a promise that those who agree with God's plan for their lives get to spend time with the only true superhero; we get to walk with God himself. And if we're honest with ourselves, this shouldn't be a hard sell since our track record isn't very good when we try to do things on our own.

PRINCIPLE 6: COMPETE

From the moment he gives us his Spirit, we begin to display the same character as Christ. We become more loving, more joyful, more peaceful, patient, and kind. We display more goodness. We welcome accountability along with a desire to help others.

Yes, no one is immediately perfect in any of these areas. That's what the Bible means when it says that we *are being transformed* into the image of Christ. It's the process whereby God begins to root out all of the garbage and replace it with the fruit of his Spirit.

Not to be too repetitive, but once I began to see that God's Spirit was living in me, I realized that my body was now the temple of God's Spirit. My body wasn't where he went to worship. Instead, it's where he went to *be* worshipped.

This is one of the reasons Kim and I decided to make some serious changes in how we treat our bodies. God lives in us, and we want to honor him by taking care of what he's given us.

One of the changes we made was to completely avoid the abuse of alcohol. And one of the reasons we made that decision is that we had seen how too much alcohol made some people think they were bigger, stronger, meaner, or funnier than they really were.

Another reason we chose not to drink too much is that I had known more than one person in Sunnyside back in the day who had destroyed their health by overindulging in liquor, beer, and wine. It was often a long, slow progression where alcohol robbed them of their dignity and work ethic. Often, after years of trying to numb the pain, they wound up frail and debilitated. Their livers and kidneys were shot. They had alienated everyone who ever loved them, and they died lonely and afraid.

I talked about this before, but Kim and I also began to do our own research on which wholesome foods were available to us. We cut

VISUALIZE YOUR GREATNESS

down on portions. And we also committed to getting our heart rates up every day by exercising.

In part, our motivation was avoiding damage to ourselves, but the real reason we changed how we treated our bodies was just what I said before. Once God began to live in us, our bodies didn't even really belong to us anymore; they belonged to God.

It wasn't easy for me. I had been raised on a diet of fatback pork, greasy pork chops, and lots of corn bread. I have no idea how many loaves of Mrs. Baird's white bread I consumed when I was a boy. We still occasionally eat those foods, but only very occasionally. We changed our diet to reflect our commitment to honor God's temple.

Even though our motivation to change what we consumed was done to honor God, when we treated God's temple with the respect it deserves, it also paid incredible dividends back to us. We now have more energy, more mental sharpness, and just generally feel better. But more than that, we believe that we are in partnership with God, honoring him by honoring the temple he lives in—our bodies. By competing for our health, we are competing for his presence.

Maybe you are thinking that it would take too much to rehabilitate your physical body, that there's too much water under the bridge. You've consumed too much alcohol, eaten too many greasy burgers, and guzzled down too many sugary drinks. Your cholesterol is off the charts, along with your blood sugar. Maybe it's been years since you walked any farther than the short distance to your mailbox.

In one sense, you may be correct. Perhaps you have done some damage. Maybe even a lot of it. But there's one thing you can't deny: No matter how much damage you've done to your body, the only way to avoid doing more is to make serious changes in how you treat it. I haven't met a person yet who couldn't make drastic improvements to their physical health by making a few modifications to their daily routine.

Yes, it can be hard. But this is what I am talking about when I say that successful people compete for their health. The unhealthiest people I've known also wished they were healthy. But, once again, this is another of those areas of life that don't simply happen to us. We have to fight for health, both mental and physical, and the two are often tied together.

Good health is always preceded by a firm commitment to compete for it by taking one hard step at a time. If you begin to do that, I'll make a promise to you. Before too long, the steps won't be as hard as they were at first. And then, after a while, your pursuit of better health becomes like muscle memory to you.

3. COMPETE TO STAY YOUNG AT HEART

At the moment, I am in my mid-sixties. To be honest, when I was a young man growing up in Sunnyside, most people I knew who were sixty years old seemed ancient to me. Many of them had, unfortunately, spent a lifetime living hard and giving little thought to the damage they were doing to their bodies and minds.

I don't blame them. For one thing, as tough as life was for a young guy like me coming of age in the seventies and early eighties, it was far more difficult for the older generation. They had seen far more injustice and poverty than kids my age had.

Life is hard for a lot of folks, just living from paycheck to paycheck. So, when we talk about staying young at heart, that can seem almost impossible when you're struggling to feed hungry bellies, keep a roof over your head, and keep the bill collector from knocking on your front door.

VISUALIZE YOUR GREATNESS

But as I think back to those early days in Sunnyside, I can clearly remember listening to the stories that some of the older people told. We didn't have cable news at the time. In fact, the only time we got any news at all was early in the morning or later afternoon, when the local television stations broadcast it for a few minutes.

What we did have instead was the Sunnyside grapevine, where bad news was passed from one person or group to another in cafés and churches and on the street corner where old men and women would pull up a chair to talk about current events.

I can't overstate the negative impact those "news" stories had on some people. Just like people being addicted to cable news today, the stories that were told made dreams seem impossible. It wasn't that the stories they told were totally untrue; it was that when they repeatedly recounted how racism and poverty had robbed them of opportunity, that story became more powerful than the one they should have heard in church—that Jesus came to give abundant life to anyone who follows him. He offers us the opportunity to live an exuberant and youthful life.

I am well aware of the fact that there is more than enough bad news to go around, and a lot of it is real. Racism in the sixties was real. In fact, it was the law. While the headlines are different today, they are still almost all negative. Just now, I took a peek at a couple of news websites and found all the negativity I could ever want to see. If bad news, rumors, conspiracy theories, and negativity are the bulk of my mental diet, I'll grow old way before my time.

I'm aware of what's in the news. I am also well aware of the ugliness of our history. But I have chosen to live in the present with a confident expectation that my future will be good. That's why I am inspired by older people who accomplished things most of us would not expect from folks who are approaching their "golden" years.

PRINCIPLE 6: COMPETE

Take a look at these "old" people:

- Frank Dobesh (fifty-seven years old)—competed in his first hundred-mile bike ride ten years after he had been diagnosed with an inoperable brain tumor

- Satchel Paige (fifty-eight years old)—became the oldest Major League Baseball player

- J. R. R. Tolkien (sixty-two years old)—published the first volume of his fantasy series *The Lord of the Rings*

- Noah Webster (sixty-six years old)—completed writing *An American Dictionary of the English Language*

- Ed Whitlock (sixty-nine years old)—became the oldest person to run a sub-three-hour marathon with a time of 2:52:47

- Katsusuke Yanagisawa (seventy-one years old)—a retired Japanese school teacher; became the oldest person to climb Mount Everest

- Margaret Ringenberg (seventy-two years old)—flew around the world

- Barbara Hillary (seventy-five years old)—one of the oldest people, and the first Black woman, to reach the North Pole

- John Glenn (seventy-seven years old)—became the oldest person to go to space

- William Ivy Baldwin (eighty-two years old)—celebrated turning eighty-two by crossing the South Boulder Canyon in Colorado on a wire 125 feet above the ground

- Allan Stewart (ninety-one years old)—completed a Bachelor of Laws degree from the University of New England

153

VISUALIZE YOUR GREATNESS

- Paul Spangler (ninety-two years old)—finished his fourteenth marathon

- Keiko Fukuda (ninety-eight years old)—became the first woman to ever attain a tenth-degree black belt, judo's highest honor

- Teiichi Igarashi (ninety-nine years old)—climbed Mount Fuji

I don't think these people are any more extraordinary than you and me. They simply had extraordinary attitudes and mindsets that empowered them to compete to stay young. That's what I have committed to doing. Hopefully, you'll join me.

See you at the finish line!

4. COMPETE IN RELATIONSHIPS

When I was a student at Crispus Attucks Middle School, I learned an invaluable lesson about the importance of genuine relationships.

I've mentioned my friend Ron Williams already. I met him when we were in the fourth grade at Sunnyside Elementary School. Ron and I were a lot alike. Neither of us were at all the kind of flashy kid who would have a posse of boys wanting to soak up our coolness. We were both kind of quiet and content to hang out in the shadows of the elementary school culture.

But, as good as our friendship is today, it almost ended before it even began. One day, we were playing a softball game at Sunnyside Elementary. When it was my turn at the plate, I took a hard swing at the ball, sending it into the outfield. I rounded first and slid into second base. Ron's best friend, Carlos, yelled, "*Out!* I tagged him!"

PRINCIPLE 6: COMPETE

I knew I was safe. No doubt about it. But Carlos puffed out his chest, waved his arms in the air, and continued his protest, "I'm saying you're out, Singletary!"

Ron stepped in and supported Carlos's version of the play. So, I puffed out my chest too, turned to him, and said, "You can get some of this too, if you want it." I was ready to throw down! Looking back on it, I now see how my emerging testosterone levels got the best of me.

Now, I'm sure if Carlos and Ron even remember that day, their version of the story might be entirely different. But I'm sure Ron recalls what happened later exactly as I do.

Afterward, we began to have a conversation and realized that we actually had a lot in common. We've been the best of friends ever since.

I think our closeness was forged, in part, because of the circumstances we shared. Both of us grew up in families characterized by a generous amount of hell. Both of us had lost brothers in automobile accidents. Ron became a part of my family, to be honest. Later, he began working with my father, brothers, and me in our family business.

A few years later, when we were students together at Crispus Attucks Middle School in Sunnyside, a new student (we'll call him Johnnie) enrolled in our class. Looking at him as he sauntered through the hallways, going from class to class, you just knew he was the coolest kid in school. Good-looking and athletic, he was soon named the quarterback of the football team. Before too long, he was the most popular kid in school. All the girls loved him, and all the guys wanted to be just like him. He had it all.

I'm ashamed to admit it now, but something in me compelled me to line up with all the other guys who wanted to be best friends with Johnnie. For one thing, he seemed to know everything. Whenever gossip made its rounds through the hallways of our school, Johnnie

155

VISUALIZE YOUR GREATNESS

always seemed to have the inside scoop before any of the rest of us even heard the rumblings.

I wish I had seen it then, but I later discovered that Johnnie was usually lying—he was not nearly as confident as he seemed. In fact, he was insecure to the extreme.

But at the time, I didn't know this. So, I did what I had to do to keep my friendship with him. I followed him around like a puppy, accepting the little morsels of "friendship" that he tossed my way. I tried to emulate his laugh, his walk, and the lines he used to meet girls and make new friends. And worst of all, I laughed at his stupid and often cruel jokes, even when I was the target of his twisted sense of humor.

I don't remember what grade we were in, but I do remember we all agreed to a pickup basketball game after school one day. We had a time-honored way of choosing team captains. We all lined up and took a shot. The first two guys to make it had the first pick of the players.

I walked up to the line, took my shot, and *whoosh*! Nothing but net.

I chose Johnnie, even though I had always chosen Ron before. Sadly, I almost ruined a great friendship. I could see the hurt in Ron's face. He lowered his shoulders, walked slowly off the court, and disappeared behind the athletic building. He never returned.

My conscience bothered me so much that I couldn't even enjoy the game, so I left soon after Ron did. Later, in the confines of my bedroom, I reflected on what I had done. I had hurt Ron. But he wasn't the only one wounded. I had hurt my own feelings too. If Ron was disappointed in me, I was more disappointed in myself.

I spoke out loud to myself, "What is going on inside of you, Mike? Why did you choose that 'pretend friend' over a friend who's been like a brother to you for years?"

PRINCIPLE 6: COMPETE

I didn't like the answer! I chose Johnnie because I thought choosing him would give me clout with my peers. If I could be seen as a close friend of Johnnie's, then maybe I could have the same kind of following that he did.

That's the day I found out what true friendships were all about. When hanging out with Johnnie, I did all the work. I call it *work* because it was all about him and what his associates could bring to his table.

What really cut me to the bone was when I recalled the words my mother had spoken over me years before: "A friend is always there, even when you're at your worst moment. He's always for you, even when you're wrong. He may even tell you that you're wrong, but he'll still be there."

As a result of my self-reflection, I began to take a fresh look at both Johnnie and Ron. My friendship with Ron was based on mutual encouragement, burden bearing, and accountability. The other was based on Johnnie using me like a pawn while I used him like a stepping stone to create a new (but fake) public persona. One relationship was phony, while the other was real.

The very next day, I walked past Johnnie in the cafeteria and went straight to Ron's table to sit with him. And for the rest of our time together in middle school, and even into high school, I did the same thing every day. I sat with Ron.

Enduring friendships that last as many years as my relationship with my brother Ron don't just happen. Ours was forged as we walked together through the intense heat of life's challenges. We've buried a brother together and celebrated life together, too. We've mourned death and celebrated life. All of it has brought us closer together.

5. COMPETE FOR HONESTY WITH OUR KIDS

Before I get too far into this section, let me get something straight. I am grateful for my career in the NFL. It was nothing short of phenomenal. But as good as all of that was, nothing about it ever came close to what I've experienced being Kim's husband and the father of my children.

The problem was, as I've said, that none of that came naturally to me. It wasn't long after Kim and I were married that I found out I had no clue what being a good husband looked like because the example my father set was so flawed. The same can be said about my preconceptions about what a father should be like. My dad was not good at that either. Neither was his father, or his father either.

So, I have had to fight like crazy to discover what it means to be a family man. In fact, I'm still fighting to be a better husband, father, and grandfather than I was the day before.

But even though I have grown a great deal in these important roles, I did have one desire before I ever even met Kim. I wanted my kids to know that I would lay down my life for them. My goal was to equip them for life in ways that I had not been. I wanted to help them avoid the pitfalls that had almost tripped me up a time or two along the way.

I was aware of the desire that almost everyone has to protect their image. I had the same desire, too. But when it came to my kids, I figured that if I was going to help them avoid traveling the same hard way I did, then I would have to be honest about how I had stumbled along the way.

For example, I shared with them that I lied a lot as a kid. It wasn't something I was proud of, but there were two reasons they needed to know that I lied. One is that I wanted to teach them that lying never

PRINCIPLE 6: COMPETE

really got me out of trouble. In fact, it always made things worse for me, and this would produce the same outcome for them.

The other reason I wanted to let them know about my past as a professional liar was that I wanted them to be keenly aware that I knew all the tricks. Because I had been so good at it, I could tell when they were lying.

But one of the hardest things about being a parent is that we realize that the apple sometimes doesn't fall too far from the tree. Man, they were good! Almost as good at lying as I was. However, each one of them had something that gave them away.

My son Matt would just keep changing the subject until you found yourself on a rabbit trail of nonsense. "No, that's not what I'm talking about! What do you mean? No, I didn't mean that, Dad! That was something totally different!"

When he launched into diversions, I knew he was lying. I told him, "Son, that's good, but you forget you are talking to the master. Make it easy on yourself and confess while you're still ahead."

My daughter Jill, our third child, had a telltale nose twitch, like from the old television show *Bewitched*, when she was lying. Our fourth child, Jackie, had body language that would give it away. She didn't say much, but she was really good at playing crazy when she lied.

Once all seven of them were old enough to understand, I gathered them all together one day and said, "Dad's got something he wants to tell you about." I had them all sit in front of me in a semicircle so that I could look each of them in the eye, and I began to let them know just how broken my childhood had been. I told them that all seven of them combined weren't as bad as I was when I was a kid.

I shared with them how I had been the classic latchkey kid, and how I would run home from school to an empty house. I recounted

159

VISUALIZE YOUR GREATNESS

how I would throw my books on the couch and run to the park, where I would play until dark.

I confessed how, since I was often unsupervised, I often chose to hang out with bad characters. I even told them about the four hoodlums I told you about earlier, with whom I spent way too much time. Since they were also latchkey kids, we had plenty of time to find foolish things to do.

I told them about the times the five of us walked the mile or so to the dump and swam in the filthy retention pond with snakes slithering across the surface of the rancid water. I never let my parents know about that because, had they known, it's safe to say I would have had lasting memories of that punishment.

I was a little uncomfortable telling my children all of this, but it was important to me to let my kids know that whatever mistakes and foolish choices they made would never be as bad as the choices I had made early in my life. I also wanted them to know that no sin of theirs would be so egregious that they couldn't come to Kim and me and confess, because we (especially me) had also done some really dumb things when we were younger. We wanted the kids to know that they weren't bad people when they messed up; they had simply made bad choices, just like their daddy had done.

By confessing my own failures and moral shortcomings, I hoped to diffuse the pressure they might be feeling to live up to impossible expectations.

I really wanted our kids to know the truth about their dad, and that even though he spoke at churches, counseled men, and led Bible studies, it was because of his keen awareness of the grace he had received (and continued to receive) that he could speak to others about God with a straight face.

PRINCIPLE 6: COMPETE

More than anything, I wanted them to know that God's love for them had nothing to do with their goodness any more than my love for them did. And because God loved me so fully, even while I was an unrepentant sinner, I loved them that way too. I let them know that, while I passionately wanted them to live a holy life and be aware of God's love for them, I would never love them less, no matter what they did.

These days I don't give my kids a lot of advice, but if they ask me about where I came from or even what my current struggles are, I will always tell them the truth.

It wasn't easy creating a culture of honesty in our family. But our love for them was (and still is) so intense that we were willing to viciously compete for their souls. Whatever it took, we were willing to do it, even if it meant being completely open about our failures, both past and present. The way we see it, our kids are more important than our image. If telling them about how we failed would give them the tools to avoid the same mistakes, it was worth it.

6. COMPETE TO MAKE A DIFFERENCE

I may have mentioned it, but I'm going to say it again—my mama sure could cook. So, when she said that we were going to pack a picnic lunch to take to the park for the Fourth of July celebration, I was pretty fired up. I began drooling when she gave the order, "Mikey, tote these dishes to the car. Be careful and don't drop them."

There was a boatload of crispy fried chicken, potato salad, green beans, and pound cake, along with a bunch of other good food. It was one of those things that, once it's over, you can hardly believe it even happened.

VISUALIZE YOUR GREATNESS

The celebration began with such promise. We were having the time of our lives—joking, laughing, playing ball, and the kids all chasing one another in a never-ending game of tag.

Then, it came out of nowhere, sort of like one of those summer thunderstorms that blow in from the Gulf of Mexico in the hot Texas summers. Without warning, my sister and brother-in-law began to scream and argue with one another at the top of their voices. It didn't even start small—it just exploded. One minute, everything was fine, and the next, they looked like they were going to throw punches.

Mama finally ordered everyone back in the car. So, we loaded up our belongings and headed home. You would think that in the short time it took to get back to the house, tempers would have cooled. But no, not in the Singletary family. They just picked up where they had left off.

As I said, I hated fighting, so I briefly retreated to the inside of the house while the rest of the crew went straight to the backyard, where it all began all over again. Only this time, my mom, my siblings, and the rest of the family were all on one side of the yard, and my brother-in-law was on the other.

I could see that, this time, the argument was even more volatile than it had been in the park. That's when I did the unthinkable. I slowly walked outside, past my family, and stood shoulder to shoulder with my sister's husband. I said loudly enough for everyone to hear, "I saw the whole thing unfold, from the beginning until we left the party." I pointed like a prosecutor identifying the guilty perpetrator in court and said, "Sis, you were the one who was wrong!" I then put my hand down by my side and shut my mouth.

Man, you could have heard a pin drop. No one said a word until my mother spoke up. "Mikey, what are you doing? Do you realize that you're going against your family? You don't ever do that, son!"

162

I didn't respond. I just stood there silently, confident that I'd done the right thing. One by one, they all retreated into the house. No one said another word. They knew I was right.

Later that night, the rest of the family assembled in the living room. They had no idea that I was close enough to hear them. Suddenly, one of them broached the subject everyone was apparently thinking about.

"What's wrong with Michael?" one of them asked. "You can't go against your family, your blood." They spent a lot of the next few minutes discussing how I had disappointed them by taking my brother-in-law's side, but no one said a thing about whether I was telling the truth.

I learned a big lesson that day: Doing the right thing often means that you will do it alone.

This lesson came in handy another time, not long afterward. When I was in middle school, someone thought that it would be a good idea to integrate Crispus Attucks Middle School. The day came for the White kids to make their appearance. The bus pulled up to the bus loop at our school, and two White kids, who appeared to be brother and sister, tentatively stepped onto the sidewalk.

I had seen footage of Black kids who were the first to integrate into White schools before. I saw the White students spit on them, ridicule them, and hit them with their fists and other objects. But I had never seen it in reverse. Naively, I supposed that, because we had been subjected to that kind of treatment, we would never do the same to another human being.

I was wrong! Some of the Black students circled around these two terrified kids and began to taunt and threaten them. I could see the sheer terror in their eyes.

VISUALIZE YOUR GREATNESS

I'm not going to lie, I was afraid to act, but I did act despite my fears. I stepped forward and stood in front of the two frightened White children and said at the top of my voice, "Stop! Stop it right now! This isn't right! If anyone else tries to hurt these kids again, they'll have to go through me first."

Thankfully, a few of my classmates stepped forward in solidarity with me, and I escorted the kids to the principal's office myself. "We're just not ready yet," I said to the principal.

I never saw those kids again.

This is what making a difference means. We must compete against prejudices and hatred. It means turning our backs on our fears when we know that we have been uniquely positioned to do something that makes a difference.

Is it hard? Yes! It's difficult to stand alone in the moment. But what's harder is living with the knowledge that we could have done the right thing but chose not to for fear that we would be rejected by others.

7. CELEBRATE YOUR VICTORIES, BUT COMPETE TO EXPERIENCE MORE

It was 1986, and we had just won the Super Bowl for the 1985 season. I was sitting in the locker room after the game, reflecting on the season—what a year! What a team! All the drama and excitement one could ask for!

I wanted to take it all in, everything—the competition on the turf, the tape from wrapped ankles and elbows, the blood from scrapes and scratches and hard hits.

I suddenly realized that I was alone; all the other guys had left the locker room high-fiving and slapping one another on the back. It was now just me and my thoughts. My mind went to the night

PRINCIPLE 6: COMPETE

before, when Coach Ditka had asked seven or eight of us what we were going to do to contribute to the victory. I also thought about the rumor I had confirmed, that our defensive coordinator, Buddy Ryan, was thinking about leaving. I couldn't imagine how that was possible.

And finally, I thought about my beautiful wife, who was carrying our first child.

The rest of my teammates were talking about the party that would take place the next day in Chicago, but I was meditating on something else. I had told Kim that, after the game, I wanted to skip the party and fly straight to Hawaii so that I could spend my time casting a vision for our team for the next year. I had a question that only I could answer: What do I need to do to put our team in a position to repeat as Super Bowl champions in the 1986 season? I needed to reflect on that while the experience was fresh in my mind.

But there was something more important that I needed to think about too. Since my father's example wasn't what I envisioned for my family, I had a lot to contemplate if I was going to break the Singletary chain of bad fatherhood. I knew that if I was going to grow into my primary role as father and husband, it would have to be an intentional growth that was fueled by the Word of God. God had promised me that he would lead me in those areas, but I knew I had to submit to his wisdom and not rely on my own instincts.

Don't get me wrong—the Super Bowl win was an incredible experience. I still like to talk about it. But that night in the locker room, I knew that I didn't want to let that win define the rest of my life.

I had already seen plenty of guys who reached the pinnacle of success, only to stop and live on that one small mountaintop for the rest of their lives. I remembered some of my Baylor University teammates, who were still talking about the 1980 season when we won the Southwest Conference title (when there was still a Southwest

VISUALIZE YOUR GREATNESS

Conference). Even some of my teammates from Worthing High School were still living in the fading glory of what we did when we were teenagers. All of them reached a point of success and just stopped right there. They never moved on.

I think about that from time to time. What if I had just stopped and rested on the glory of January 26, 1986? What if that had become how I defined my life? "I am Mike Singletary, a member of the 1986 Super Bowl championship team!"

Would I have enjoyed all the other successes that I've had? Would I still be married to Kim? Would I have these incredible, accomplished kids who bring me more joy than I could have ever imagined? Would I have the personal and life-changing relationship with my Heavenly Father that guides my every step today? Would I have allowed myself to fail and experience the growth that comes from failing?

I can answer those questions for you. *No!* I would not! I would be like so many other players and people in other fields who reached a mountaintop and stopped, living in the glory of yesterday. I don't know how many men and women I've known who did that. They're still boasting about what they did in 1986, but for me, it's sobering to think that 1986 was almost forty years ago. Most people who are under fifty years old don't even remember who Mike Singletary is. If our Super Bowl victory was the only good thing I'd ever done, what good would that do me now?

On that night all those years ago, I knew that my life did not consist of the abundance of my possessions, nor of the list of my past accomplishments on the turf. I knew that there had to be more, but the only reason I knew that was because Jesus had already told me so (Luke 12:15). I had to keep on growing and moving forward by the power of God's Spirit.

Today? Well, I can tell you with a straight face that I'm excited to throw the covers back every morning and rise up to live the day. I'm fired up about what I'm learning and the opportunity to make my life valuable.

I'm not claiming to be perfect. I certainly have flaws! My wife and kids can testify to that. But what I can tell you is that I live in the expectation that I will grow as a man who follows Christ.

One of the practices that has kept me honest about my growth and fueled my desire for more victories is that I daily ask myself a series of questions that have served me well over the years. I would encourage anyone who wants to move on from the past and live in the present, desiring an infinite future, to borrow them for their own use:

- Are you making your time valuable?

- Are you excited about what you're going to do?

- Is anyone asking to meet with you for breakfast because they see God working in your life and they want the same thing?

- Are your conversations current and relevant, or are you only talking about the past?

- Are you aware that God's still, quiet voice is speaking to you, or did you turn it off at some time in the past? Are you running on autopilot?

As I said, I've known plenty of men who were incredibly successful competing on the football field only to be abysmal failures in almost every other area of their lives. I'm talking about Heisman Trophy winners, players who were All-Pro or Hall of Famers. Many of them shared my commitment to competition, except they were

VISUALIZE YOUR GREATNESS

shortsighted and relentlessly competed in only one arena: sports. In almost every other area of their lives, it was a bust.

God has blessed me beyond measure. I have been able to have a lifestyle that my parents and most of the citizens of Sunnyside never enjoyed or even dreamed possible.

But I shudder to think about what my life would have been like had I put on the brakes after football. What if I had stopped competing for more victories in the more important areas of my life? What if I had not radically competed for my marriage? What if I had not fought for my kids? What if I had not competed to continue to hear God's voice and committed myself to obeying him? What would have become of me had I refused to admit my failures in those relationships and turned back to God's purpose for me?

I shudder to think about it because I am certain that my life would be much different from what it is now, and not in a good way.

You and I get one shot at life. For all of us, it's one day at a time. We all get the same twenty-four hours, 1,440 minutes, 86,400 seconds every single day. The question we must both answer is, "Are we investing those hours and minutes and seconds wisely, or are we drifting from one idle moment to the next?"

I pray that we can both commit to taking the gift of time and investing it wisely, intentionally fighting for more and better victories than we did the day before.

PRINCIPLE 7
COMMITTED

---

com·mit

/kəˈmit/

verb

verb: commit

1. pledge or bind (a person or an organization) to a certain course or policy.

I love the word Committed, because it's not about what you say, but what you do. All I want to know is, did you do your best when the chips were high or when they were low?

Pushing through the hard things in life, that's how you grow.
In the end, excuses are a dime a dozen,
And quitting is its first cousin—'he said, she said,' all that jugglin
And the naysayers are always buzzin.
But when you get alone, look deep with your heart;
You'll find that the winners, they finish what they start.

VISUALIZE YOUR GREATNESS

As you journey on the path to accomplish your goals, you will be faced with the same task over and over: Will you accept the person "they" say you are, or will you become the winner you are inside? If you let them, they will dictate the boundaries for your success: what you can and cannot do, how far you can and cannot go. But they cannot measure your heart, determination, work ethic, focus, and positive mindset. On the outside you may look small, but on the inside, you're a giant.

What they see of you is limited. What's really inside of you is not. This is the picture I see of myself.

What's inside of you?

"Greater is He who is in you than he who is in the world" (1 John 4:4)

PRINCIPLE 7: COMMITTED

1. COMMIT TO BUILDING A GREAT SELF-IMAGE

In 1993, just before my last game in the NFL, the Bears published an article about me in their newsletter. They were interviewing my teammates about what kind of man and player I had been. I guess it was their way of saying goodbye to me.

Some of the guys responded by saying things such as, "He's really different!" (I didn't know whether to be flattered or insulted.) "He doesn't swear! He doesn't cheat!"

I was good with all of that, but at least one of them also said something that I didn't completely agree with. He said, "He's a bad athlete! He's not the fastest guy in the world! He's not the biggest guy in the world! He couldn't even beat Buddy Ryan at racquetball."

OK, let me set the Buddy Ryan racquetball story straight. This is the way it really happened.

I showed up one day at the racquetball court only to find out that it was just Buddy and me. He pointed his finger and commanded me, "Samurai, it's you and me."

I wouldn't say that I was afraid to play him, but I will admit to being a little apprehensive about the prospect of getting inside the four walls of the court with him. For one thing, I didn't have a relationship with him at the time. In fact, I already felt like he didn't like me.

So, yes, I was intimidated by him. Worse than that, however, was that Buddy had a reputation for not exactly playing by the rules. I soon found out just how competitive he was. He slammed me against the wall, hit me with his racquet, and popped me in the back with that blue ball more than once.

He did beat me. I didn't even want to win. Winning was the last thing on my mind. I just wanted to walk off the court in one piece.

I don't know if the guys really thought I was a "bad" athlete or not, but I think the bigger point they were trying to make was

VISUALIZE YOUR GREATNESS

that I practiced and played far above my physical ability. Like Clark Kent and Superman, or maybe the Incredible Hulk, I went through a metamorphosis of sorts once I strapped on my pads. I was suddenly transformed from an average-size guy with decent speed to a guy who played like he was special.

To give you a clear view of my two personae, I need to tell you what Mike Ditka said about me: "Mike's always in the corner reading his Bible."

He told the truth. I did read my Bible a lot, even in the locker room. But if that's all you knew about me, you would have a hard time realizing that Mike Singletary, the Bible reader, was the same guy as Number 50, who lined up at middle linebacker.

That's why it's kind of ironic that I became known as Samurai Mike. My teammate Doug Plank was the first one to hang that moniker on me. The reason he began to call me that is that, during practice and games, I would line up and make sounds like those that Bruce Lee made just before he knocked his opponents out—a series of high-pitched squeals and grunts.

Looking back on it, I guess it was a little over the top. But the fact that I wasn't normally loud or even outgoing added to the mystique. I wanted the offensive players to know that Mike Singletary was fully committed to getting better. I often told my teammates, "I'm not going half speed." The most important thing for me as the middle linebacker was to be the example—full speed, every play.

I saw Doug Plank a while back, and as we reminisced about our days with the Bears, he told me, "I loved watching your energy! Mike, how did you play with such energy all the time?" I told him that, when I was young, I had decided to always go full speed, all out, all the time. I had asked God to bless me and give me favor, and my

PRINCIPLE 7: COMMITTED

job had been to always give my best, to never take a play off. And I believed that in doing that, God would honor me.

I'm not sure how much the other guys looked forward to practice, but I loved it. By the time I got there, I was so well prepared that I couldn't wait to begin. I believed that if I honored God in practice, he would honor me on game day.

Buddy Ryan always said that football was 90 percent mental and 10 percent physical. In my opinion, it's more like 75 percent mental and 25 percent physical. Either way, most players never got that, and I didn't either until later in life. However, as I think back on my days playing, I realize that I had an expectation to make every play, not because I was better but because I had rehearsed every play over and over in my mind. I was so prepared that I knew what was going to happen before it happened. Sometimes, I even thought to myself, *How did I know that was going to happen?* That's when I began to understand the power of the subconscious mind.

It may sound arrogant for me to say that this was my image of myself. And honestly, it would be if it were an image I had conjured up by my own power. But that's not what I did. Instead, what I thought about myself was what God said about me. I knew that he loved me. But more than that, I was certain that he wanted to honor my desire to bring glory to his name.

So, when I played well and we won, I honored him. I gave God all the glory. When I failed and we lost, I honored him then, too, by taking responsibility for my failure to prepare and execute.

This is why I never felt better or worse about myself when the guys teased me about being a Bible reader, or when I made a mistake on the field, or when the coaches were hard on me. Even all these years later, my self-image doesn't change based on my circumstances.

Even when I become aware of ways that I've failed Kim or the kids, for example, it doesn't change anything. I know that God loves me.

That's because who I am is not really tied to what I do or to what someone else thinks of me. The only thing that really matters is God's opinion of me. And he says that I bear his image and that I am his son. The best part of God's promise is that this father–son relationship is irrevocable.

This is the foundation of my life. More than anything else, it is who I am. It is a safe relationship because of the permanence of my Father's love for me. If I left him, shook my fist in his face, and told him that I hated him, he may not bless me. I may lose the blessing of his presence. I may lose my joy and peace. He may even discipline me. I can't be presumptuous and take his grace for granted and live in rebellion against him! But if I want him, I can easily have him; however, I must repent of my rebellion and learn to rely on him again, to trust that he's truthful with me. But one thing never changes in the middle of all this: While he hates sin, he will continue to love me, and he still offers forgiveness if I repent.

I didn't make this up. It's what God's Word says about me:

And so we know and rely on the love God has for us. God is love. Whoever lives in love lives in God, and God in them. This is how love is made complete among us so that we will have confidence on the day of judgment: In this world we are like Jesus. There is no fear in love. But perfect love drives out fear, because fear has to do with punishment. The one who fears is not made perfect in love. (1 John 4:16–18)

Do you see how this differs from the worldly kind of self-image that relies on "Do better! Perform more! Hide your mistakes! Protect yourself by blaming others!"?

PRINCIPLE 7: COMMITTED

Rather than relying on my performance for my self-image, I am learning to rely on God's love for me instead. This is way better. And it's why I don't think I'm arrogant at all because my confidence doesn't come from me. It comes from God's love for me.

Because of his love, I am like Jesus in the world. People see God working in me. They know that my love for others is based entirely on the example of God, who loved me first (1 John 4:19). Furthermore, they know that my desire to be obedient to God is rooted in my faith in the truthfulness of what Jesus said: "The wages of sin is death!" (Rom. 6:23)

While I did take a fair amount of ribbing, and I'm sure a bit of chitchat behind my back from my teammates about my love for God, I think that's why so many of them would come to me in private and confess, "Mike, I'm having trouble in my relationship. Can you help me? Will you pray with me?"

My love for God was very public; I never tried to hide it from anyone. It was so public, in fact, that when some of the guys threw one of those lavish parties some athletes are famous for, my wife and I were sometimes not invited. I guess they thought I was too boring. I get it—having a Bible-banger who's serious about his relationship with God is a buzzkill in some settings.

Looking back on it, I wish I could have been more of an extrovert. One of the things about my childhood I had to overcome was that, because of all the trauma from a tough childhood, the social piece just wasn't there. Sometimes, it looks like I am in a bad mood when I'm just as happy as I can be on the inside.

I'm grateful that God gave me a wife who is unafraid to call me out when I'm falling short in areas like this. Without any reluctance at all, Kim challenges me about the vibes my facial expression gives off. More than once, she's said something like, "Mike, you have to

VISUALIZE YOUR GREATNESS

practice smiling. You're a believer, but you're scaring people. You look like you're in a bad mood."

Thank God for a wife like her who knows what's really in my heart. I don't know, maybe that's the real reason the guys didn't hang around with me as much as they did one another. Maybe I was sending the wrong message. But I also believe that it was in part because of my public commitment to my testimony.

If that was the reason they didn't invite me to the parties, I find it ironic that it was the same reason they sought me out when the fabric of their lives began to unravel. They reasoned, "Mike knows God! If anyone can fix the mess I've made, God can. Maybe Mike can introduce us!"

I was always happy to share my love for God. I knew that he is always ready to take in strays and adopt them into his family. Regardless of our past mistakes and our sorry track record, he never turns anyone away. And God often repairs broken relationships once we stop trying to be in control of our lives and hand over the reins to him.

But even when damage is done to our relationships that can't be undone, no one is better off running away from the God who loves them. Even when our pleading, begging, and negotiating with the ones we've wounded fails to convince them to give us another chance, we are still safer with God.

The good news is that God always honors a heart that seeks his face above all others. We can't sin so much that we are beyond the scope of his love and grace, no matter how far down the road of self-centeredness we've gone, and no matter how much damage we've done to our relationships. He always takes us in when we ask him to with a sincere heart.

With God, it's never too late.

PRINCIPLE 7: COMMITTED

This is why I always encouraged my friends to learn to obey the command of Jesus, who said, "Seek first the kingdom of God and his righteousness" (Matt. 6:33). I hadn't perfectly put this passage into practice at the time. In fact, I'm still growing in my obedience to this command even today.

I was also still learning that his command in that verse is followed by a promise: "and all these things will be added to you as well."

Whatever I or my friends were lacking—that drove us to seek satisfaction in the things of the world—would never have been filled by doing our own thing. That empty hole in our hearts can only be filled by seeking the kingdom of God and his righteousness above everything else. No amount of drugs and alcohol, fancy cars and houses, or sex can do that. The only way we can get what we need (peace of mind) is to seek him and his kingdom—first! When I do that, all of my desires are reordered to want what is in my best interest and to the glory of God.

When I seek the kingdom of God like this, it also means that I cherish his family name. I honor the name of God in how I try to live my life in obedience to him. I also honor his name by inviting others into the same family life with God that I enjoy. I honor him by never giving up. Even if I fall (and I do), I honor him by getting back up and seeking his kingdom all over again.

Yes, I had warts and flaws that anyone who knew me could easily see. I still do! But my self-image wasn't about any of that—it was all about the fact that I was loved by God, adopted by him into his family, and given his name. That's about all I had going for me, but it was enough. What else could I need?

So, the guys didn't come to me for advice because I was qualified to help them deal with their problems. They came to me because of

VISUALIZE YOUR GREATNESS

the connections I had made with the sovereign God of the universe, and they wanted in on it, even if some of them didn't take my advice.

Over the past few decades, I've decided that being viewed as odd isn't the worst thing that can happen to a man. I don't mind being Clark Kent. I have a beautiful wife, whom I've been with for over forty years. We've had issues like any other married couple, but thankfully, we've been true to our vows.

Not only that, we have seven amazing kids, who also bring me such joy that I don't even have the words to tell you about it. If you want to see the unhinged, uninhibited Mike Singletary, just come to our house when we're all together. I'm telling you; I'm a different guy.

But I enjoy those things because I know "whose" I am. I know whom I belong to and trust his promises that he will be faithful to keep them. That's my identity—my self-image.

If we aren't careful, however, our self-image can take a beating, especially if our image of ourselves is centered on ourselves and not the image God has tailor-made for us. For example, there was Coach Corky Nelson. At the time, I thought he was a tyrant. I honestly thought he hated me, and I wasn't too fond of him myself. It was only later that I realized that he had a great deal of confidence in my future. That's why he rode me like a mule. He believed in my potential.

But, at the time, I took it as a personal assault on my self-image. I thought he was telling me that I would never be great. In the midst of his screaming at me, berating me for the flaws in my execution, I came to a crossroads. I could either believe what I thought he was saying about me, or I could believe what God had already said about me and the vision I believed God had given me.

Thankfully, I chose to believe God, because if I had not, I would have never known that my coach believed in me, nor would I have experienced the success I did.

2. COMMIT TO NEVER QUITTING

Coach Oliver Brown!

I have a very short list of men who've influenced me to live the life that I have, and Coach is right at the top of the list. To this day, I love that man, even though he long ago entered into his eternal rest.

He was definitely an old-school kind of coach, not at all concerned about his players "getting in touch with their feelings." In fact, Coach Brown was quite the disciplinarian. Every day, he brought a wooden paddle to practice, and when anyone made a mistake, he would light up their behinds with a firm swat.

Some of the guys couldn't handle it. They would respond with some version of, "Hey, I'm a grown man! Ain't nobody gonna whip my behind." I saw more than one of them throw their helmets and pads on the field, stiffen their arms, bow up, arch their backs, and walk away. They quit before they ever tasted the sweetness of success.

Even back then, I thought about it differently. In fact, I told a few of them, "If you don't want to get paddled, do the play correctly the first time."

Most of those guys were raised by single moms and old grand-mothers who had done the best they could. Few of them had had a dad in the home. As dysfunctional as my relationship with my father was, at least I had a father. His version of what it took to be a man was very flawed, no doubt about that. But one thing Reverend Charles Singletary taught me was the value of the reward that comes from doing whatever it takes to get the job done.

I've often wondered what some of those guys would say now if someone were to ask them, "Do you wish that you had stuck it out and learned to practice until you could run the play with perfection?" I don't recall that I've ever spoken with any of them about that, but

VISUALIZE YOUR GREATNESS

I've encountered numerous other people over the years who expressed their deep regret that they had quit when the going got tough.

I'm not defending Coach Brown's practice of paddling players, except to say that most of us knew that he cared about us. He wanted to win games, but more than that, he wanted to help us break the chains of generational failure that kept so many of my teammates from entering manhood. He knew that if he could help us get over the hurdle of the temptation to quit when the going got tough, we could make it in life.

And the reason he knew about how quitting can be a destructive generational thing was because of his own family's culture. Growing up in East St. Louis, he knew all about poverty and the nasty residue that can take up residence in a young person's mind. East St. Louis was a lot like Sunnyside.

But he also realized early on that his only way out of the ghetto was to pursue an education. So, that's what he did. He majored in math at Texas Southern University, graduated, and started his career teaching school. I know firsthand that Coach Brown's greatest desire was to make a difference in as many kids' lives (kids like he had been back in East St. Louis) as he could.

When he died in 2013, the accolades poured in from his former athletes and students. They described him as a "father figure," a "role model," and a "motivator." Every life he touched at Worthing High School was fundamentally changed for the better by his loving discipline. His impact on his students was so well-known that the Texas legislature recognized his contributions to Sunnyside when it passed Resolution No. 1044 that honored the life of my mentor and friend.

Was Coach Brown intimidating?

I later became friends with NFL Hall of Famer Cliff Branch, who had graduated before I became a student at Worthing. Cliff was

PRINCIPLE 7: COMMITTED

a funny guy who could make anyone laugh. For the rest of Cliff's life, he would start out with the same funny joke every time we ran into one another, "SingSing (his nickname for me), Coach Brown coming! Coach Brown coming!"

When we had been students at Worthing, that would have been the only prompt we needed to stop our foolishness and run.

Yes, we all had a certain amount of fear when it came to Coach Brown, but more than that, we respected him because we knew he was always in our corner. He always wanted the best for us, so much so that he was willing to give us the discipline that many of my teammates lacked at home.

Was he successful? Well, all I can tell you is that he is the only high school coach I know of who has coached three players who went on to be inducted into the NFL Hall of Fame. Besides me, Cliff Branch was not only a Hall of Famer, but he was also a three-time Super Bowl champion for the Raiders. Otis Taylor was another of Coach Brown's players who won a Super Bowl.

He also coached close to twenty young men who went on to be all-Americans in college. He coached sprinter Debra Edwards, who competed in the 1972 and 1976 Olympics.

There were quitters, yes! And I know for a fact that every time a kid bailed out of his program, it broke Coach Brown's heart because he had such high hopes for all of them. He saw in them a potential that they couldn't even see in themselves. He had a better image of them than they had of themselves.

But I can't count the number of young people from Worthing High School who persevered under Coach Brown's discipline. They stuck it out through all the hard times, when everything around them seemed to say that it was too difficult and that they would be better off just quitting.

VISUALIZE YOUR GREATNESS

They were the ones who went on to accomplish great things. Coach was proud of that. So, in answer to the question of whether or not he was successful, I would say, "Yes! Without a doubt!" But his true success is not just measured in how many famous athletes he coached. It's in the untold numbers of young men and women he taught to succeed by believing the truth about themselves rather than the lies that culture told them.

It does break my heart that too many of my peers stopped just before achieving victory, but I am forever grateful for the example of the others who fought the good fight and found their way to the other side.

Almost everyone has cast a mental vision of a better life at some point and maybe even taken a step or two in pursuit of their dream. It's an easy thing to do: "I'm going to hit the gym five days a week! I'm going to lose twenty pounds! I'm going to start saving up for a down payment on a new house! I'm going to provide for and lead my family!"

Dreaming of a better life is the easy part. Even that first step isn't all that hard. Every one of the guys who signed up to play football for Coach Brown started with a dream of being a star player. None of them said, "Tell you what I'm going to do. I'm going to try out for Worthing High School's football team, show up for a few practices, and then I'm going to quit when it gets too hard."

No one starts out that way!

Everyone I've ever known who quit too soon had one thing in common: They lacked that inner voice that says, *I will not stop, I will not quit, no matter how hard my circumstances seem. I will endure pain and discipline until I break through the barrier that has kept me from being successful my whole life.*

This kind of commitment may begin with something such as sports or business, but the real blessing comes to those who have this

PRINCIPLE 7: COMMITTED

perseverance in all the important areas of their lives. And when we are aware that the voice to keep on going comes from the God who loves us, it touches everything.

It's when we hear our own voice saying, "I will not quit on my marriage! I will not quit on my kids! I will continue to fight for my community or my nation!" that we find ourselves hearing the voice that tells us the truth about ourselves. It's when we realize that we are more than who other people say we are (or even who we say we are) that we become successful.

3. COMMIT TO TAKING OWNERSHIP OF YOUR LIFE

Trust me! If anyone could find someone to blame for his failures, it would be me. My African ancestors were bought and sold like one would buy livestock. Their "owners" had no regard for their humanity at all.

One would think that by the time I came along, America would have moved past all of that. But it hadn't. Remember me telling you about the garbage trucks on the Dump Road that threw billowing clouds of dust all through Sunnyside?

What I haven't told you about are the welfare box trucks that pulled into our neighborhood on a regular schedule. Black people, mostly mothers and grandmothers, would line up and get their monthly ration of free powdered milk and powdered eggs and dried-out block cheeses.

Yes, in one sense, they were grateful for it because it kept their kids from starving, but it was dehumanizing. I clearly recall these ladies standing with shoulders slumped in line behind other women, embarrassed because they had to hold their begging hands out for the government to fill them with a little bit of free stuff.

Maybe the people in charge of the system didn't intend for the free stuff to rob grown women of their dignity, but that was the effect. No one ever said this, but we got the message loud and clear: *You are Black. You will never prosper, but we'll make sure you stay just above the starvation line. We'll give you just enough to get by. We will also give you our garbage dump, the dust, and the wretched smells, but that's it.*

Yes, it was bad. But I'm not bitter about it now, partly because my mother and father taught me that, if I worked hard and took care of my business, I wasn't predestined to be a ward of the state. My mother said to me, "You don't have to settle for this, Mike! You can succeed!"

As flawed as my father was, I'll give him this—neither he nor my mother ever allowed me to blame the system or the White man or my circumstances for any consequences that came my way. And they definitely didn't allow me to blame others for my failures that resulted from my own lack of effort.

Somewhere along the way, Mom began to repeat the words of Jesus when he said, ***"The thief comes only to steal and kill and destroy; I have come that they may have life and have it to the full"*** *(John 10:10).*

I began to see that reliance on the shallow benevolence of the system, in addition to the story that some people in our community told one another about how the system had let us down, were the words of the Thief. He loves nothing more than to rob people of their dignity and self-worth, their work ethic, and their hope of a better future by making them victims.

But the second part of that verse, "but I have come" to bring fullness of life? That is what set me free from the temptation to believe the Thief's lies. If there was any chance that Jesus was who he claimed to be (and I now fully believe that he is), then I knew that I could trust his promise to lead me into a full and satisfying kind of life.

PRINCIPLE 7: COMMITTED

When my trust is in him and his version of my destiny, I don't need more of the things of the world. As I suggested earlier, no house, no new car, no designer clothes will satisfy me. Nor will I find it in the plastic surgeon who offers to make my butt bigger or smaller, or my lips fatter or thinner, or the skin of my face tighter and wrinkle-free. And you definitely won't find me bathing in a tub of bleach water to make my skin whiter.

If I am committed to these outward things instead of the inner change that comes from God's Spirit living in me, I'll still be the same rotten person on the inside that I've always been. I'll still do the same things I always did; I'll just look better doing them.

Once I began to trust God's promises and take responsibility for my own life, I began to make changes—big changes.

For example, some of my siblings died an early death. I heard more than one of them say something like, "Hey, Grandma didn't live that long. Dying young is in our genes, so I might as well do what I'm gonna do."

I don't know why I didn't buy their version of life, but at some point, I realized I didn't have to follow the same path, living life dreading what I could not avoid. So, I decided that I wanted to live a long and productive life, and I wanted to feel good getting there. But I also knew that if I was going to do that, I would have to be proactive—I would have to make changes.

I've already told you about this, but one of the first changes I knew I had to make was in what kinds of foods I would consume.

In addition to my diet, I began to think about the stress in my life and how that could cut years from my life. I paid attention to my sleep habits, and I also considered the people I surrounded myself with. Did they bring chaos into my life, or were they friends with

VISUALIZE YOUR GREATNESS

whom I could enjoy a peaceful, drama-free relationship? Would they love me enough to hold me accountable?

I'm telling you all of this because I want you to know that I decided that I didn't just want to live. Instead, I wanted to live well, to get the most out of life, and for my life to be abundant. And to do that, I had to decide to believe what God says about how to do it.

Not many Christian preachers talk about this, but the Bible actually warns against making food an idol. Solomon said, *"Do not join those who drink too much wine or gorge themselves on meat, for drunkards and gluttons become poor, and drowsiness clothes them in rags." (Prov. 23:20–21)*

So, to take control of my life, I had to embrace God's purpose for me. Then I had to reframe my mind. I began to rely heavily on a promise that God made to Joshua. *"Have I not commanded you? Be strong and courageous. Do not be afraid; do not be discouraged, for the Lord your God will be with you wherever you go." (Josh. 1:9)*

I saw this as a command, not an option. I figured that if this was God's plan for Joshua's life, it was also his plan for mine. But since it was a command, it wasn't just going to happen to me. I had to choose to obey it, to rely on it, and to never quit obeying it.

And I would obey it, not because I would use God like a genie in a bottle, but because of his promise that he would be with me wherever I went. He would be with me when I succeeded. But more than that, he would be with me when I stumbled and failed.

When God walks with us, and we with him, there's no need to be afraid—not of anything! Not even our failures! That's why I don't quit: God is with me.

By contrast, I also knew that everything in our culture was rooted in fear. In fact, all cultures are driven by fear to some extent. I had to reject the lie of culture that made almost everyone around me afraid,

PRINCIPLE 7: COMMITTED

and I believed God instead. My siblings feared an early death, so they just went along with the flow. Some of my peers feared racism and discrimination (which were very real), so they just lived as if there wasn't even any point in trying.

So, I also meditated on the words Jesus said to his followers just before he was crucified: *"Peace I leave with you; my peace I give you. I do not give to you as the world gives. Do not let your hearts be troubled and do not be afraid." (John 14:27)*

The bottom line is this: If we are going to commit to taking ownership of our lives and having the strength to keep going even when it seems like quitting is the most rational thing to do, it must be rooted in something more secure and reliable than just what we think or in our own strength. We must get that kind of power from a higher source, from God himself.

Is it easy to take ownership? Well, no, it's not! In fact, the pathway can often be steep and grueling. But the Bible told me, *"Let us not become weary of doing good, for at the proper time we will reap a harvest if we don't give up!" (Gal. 6:9)*

Maybe trying to live this way to see if it works is better than not trying it at all. It's a good starting place, I suppose. But if I'm going to truly "reap a harvest" of living with real purpose and meaning, at some point I'm going to have to trust God that he is going to keep his promise that he will reward me for not giving up.

I don't know if I'll reach my goal of living to be an old man, but one thing I do know: However long I live, I will live better, leave a better legacy for others to follow, and live with more joy than if I don't commit to taking ownership of my life and never quitting by the power and wisdom of God.

Who, or what, am I going to believe? That's the question. What this really boils down to is Who am I going to obey?

I can obey the voice that tells me, "You are destined to fail because the system is rigged against you, so you should just stop where you are!" Or I can surrender to the one that tells me, "Your value is infinite because I know who you are, and I am with you. Therefore, your potential is infinite! So, live that way, like I am walking with you every step of the way."

You may think that you're afraid to make this decision one way or the other. But you've already made it. There's no middle ground here. We are either believing the lie, or we are believing the truth of God's Word.

If choosing God seems impossible to you, if you think that too much water has already passed under the bridge, that it's too late for you to choose him, you need to recognize that as a lie too. Every day is a new day with a new offer from God to give you the power to take control of your life.

4. COMMIT TO THESE SEVEN WORDS AND YOUR LIFE WILL CHANGE

LOVE

We talked about love in principle 1, but I want to explore it a little more here.

We say things like, "I love hamburgers!" But what we really mean is that we *like* hamburgers. That's personal preference—it's not love.

True love, on the other hand, acts more than it's felt! It sacrifices! It is on display! It gives and sacrifices on behalf of someone else!

If you want to know what true love is, don't pay any attention to the Hollywood version. What they're selling as love is often nothing

PRINCIPLE 7: COMMITTED

more than shallow sentimentality. It's almost always driven by feelings and hormones. You'll want to stay away from that version.

If it's true love you're after, I can point you in two directions.

One is to find people in your community who actually love others sacrificially. Maybe there aren't many people around you like that. In fact, sacrificial love is so uncommon that it's difficult to find in almost all communities. But I've never been anywhere that didn't have at least a few folks who loved like that. Find those people and imitate them.

As good as human examples are, however, there's a better place to find a perfect definition of true love, and that is in the Word of God. It's a pretty concise one: *"Love is patient and kind. It does not envy or boast. Nor is it proud. It does not dishonor others, it is not self-seeking, it is not easily angered, it keeps no record of wrongs. Love does not delight in evil but rejoices with the truth. It always protects, always trusts, always hopes, always perseveres." (1 Cor. 13:4–7)*

God commanded us to love like this, but I can't simply will myself to do it. It's too hard for me to demonstrate this kind of love by my own power. The only way I can do it is to first realize that this is the perfect description of how God loves me. It's a supernatural kind of love. God is patient and kind with me. He is not proud, nor is he easily angered by me (even though I sometimes think he is). He doesn't keep a tally sheet of the things I've done wrong. And most importantly, he always protects me, always trusts in his love for me, always hopes I will submit to him, and he always keeps on working with me.

God smiles when he sees me! That's how much he loves me!

God is love, and if I'm going to love like God, I must first know God and walk with him. The more time I spend with him, the more I become like him.

Is this kind of love life-changing? You bet it is. It's the most powerful force in the universe. Someone once asked Jesus what the most important command in the Bible was.

What do you think his response was? Many people might respond by saying that it would be a command to avoid a specific sin, such as "Thou shalt not commit adultery," or "Thou shalt not get drunk." But that's not how Jesus answered the question at all. He said that the most important command was, *"'Love the Lord your God with all your heart and with all your soul and with all your mind.' This is the first and greatest commandment." (Matt. 22:37–38)*

Of all the commands in the Bible, this is number one because it is the rationale for obeying all of the others. The reason I obey God when he commands me to be faithful to Kim, for example, is that I love God. I don't steal your stuff for the simple reason that I love God. Name a command, and the reason I try hard to obey it is that I take God's love seriously.

Interestingly, Jesus went on to say that there is another command just like the most important one: *"And the second is like it: 'Love your neighbor as yourself.' All the Law and the Prophets hang on these two commandments." (Matt. 22:30–40)*

What this means is that if we are seeking the good life, the one that brings us fulfillment, we can only find it in one way: by loving God with everything in us and loving our neighbors in the same way we love ourselves.

This kind of love is so uncommon in the world that almost no one loves this way. The vast majority of the eight billion people alive on Planet Earth today do not love sacrificially. They love themselves more than they love both God and their fellow man. The result of this selfish kind of love is that most people are unhappy. They are filled with bitterness and simmering anger.

PRINCIPLE 7: COMMITTED

If it's the peace that passes understanding you're after, why not give more thought to what Jesus said in this passage? Why not ask him to teach you to love him and to love your neighbor in the same way he loves you?

INDUSTRIOUS

A few months before my father passed away, he and I took a leisurely drive together. I asked him what he remembered most about his life when he looked back on it. His answer surprised me.

Large tears formed in his sad eyes as he began to speak. "I miss my men. I handpicked every one of them. They were all great workers. If they were sick or had family issues, I never knew it. I couldn't keep those guys from working."

My mother used to say, "Work so hard that they'd miss you if you weren't there."

What I think my parents were trying to teach me is that I may have no control over what someone else says about me or how they treat me, but when it comes to how I do my job, I do have total control over how seriously I take the tasks that my employer has assigned to me. They may fire me, but they won't fire me because I didn't work harder than anyone else on the job.

MEDITATION

I've already alluded to this earlier, but I learned an important skill when I was just a boy. I didn't know then how valuable it would be to me as I grew into manhood, but I do now.

Whenever the Singletary home exploded into loud drama, I refused to take part in it. As I told you before, as the youngest child, they didn't notice when I wasn't there. So, I would sneak away to a quieter place, close my eyes, control my breathing, and hover above the noise.

Of course, I was still there physically (I was too young to leave), but in my mind, I was somewhere else, somewhere quieter and healthier. At some point, I realized that I could emotionally and spiritually remove myself from any situation so completely that I didn't even hear the busyness of what was going on around me. I couldn't hear my parents and siblings fighting. I couldn't hear the siren blaring past my bedroom window. I learned to tune it all out and concentrate on better thoughts.

For me, the benefit of this kind of meditation is that my stress levels took a nosedive. I also learned that my inner peace isn't determined by my outer circumstances as much as it is by what I turn my mind to.

According to an article published by the Mayo Clinic staff on December 14, 2023, centering your thoughts on something that calms you can give you "a sense of calm, peace, and balance that can benefit your emotional well-being" and your "overall health."[8]

The Mayo people weren't even talking about centering our thoughts on the Creator, just on happy things. Think about it—if just thinking happy thoughts can elevate our mood and give us a sense of calm and balance, how much more at peace can we be when we meditate on God?

---

8   Mayo Clinic Staff, "Stress Relievers: Tips to Tame Stress," mayoclinic.org, August 3, 2023, https://www.mayoclinic.org/healthy-lifestyle/stress-management/in-depth/stress-relievers/art-20047257#:~:text=During%20meditation%2C%20you%20focus%20your,to%20enhance%20our%20well%2Dbeing.

EXERCISE

Exercise is a true game changer. Exercise strengthens willpower, and it releases serotonin and endorphins that increase happiness, regulate stress and anxiety, and decrease depression.

Our body spends energy in three ways: digesting food, exercising, and maintaining the body's functions (e.g., the respiratory and cardiovascular systems). Exercise is good for muscles and bones, because as we age, we *lose* muscle mass and functionality.

Exercise increases our energy levels and boosts our immune systems. It is imperative, not only for our physical health but for our brain health as well. Exercise increases the size of our hippocampus, which can help to ward off chronic diseases and illnesses such as Alzheimer's disease and schizophrenia. Regular exercise can result in better sleep and have us feeling more energized during the day. It can also reduce pain, stimulate our sex life, and improve our overall quality of life.

SLEEP

Sleep is so incredibly important, but many people mistakenly wear a lack of sleep as a badge of honor.

But sleep's main function is to rid our brains of toxins and process information accumulated throughout the day. Research suggests that adults need at least seven hours of sleep each night.[9] This amount of time allows the brain to repair and rejuvenate the cells throughout the body.

---

9   Eric Olson, "How Many Hours of Sleep Do You Need?," Mayo Clinic, February 1, 2025, https://www.mayoclinic.org/healthy-lifestyle/adult-health/expert-answers/how-many-hours-of-sleep-are-enough/faq-20057898.

VISUALIZE YOUR GREATNESS

Sleeping well also helps stave off sugar cravings and helps us feel fuller after meals, aiding us in maintaining a healthy weight.[10] People who get adequate sleep have fewer struggles with anxiety and depression.

Conversely, adults who regularly sleep five hours or fewer per night are more likely to develop heart disease, type 2 diabetes, arthritis, and high blood pressure, and they are three times more likely to develop colds. A sleep-deprived person looks older, has more visible wrinkles, and has sagging and puffy eyes.

FORGIVENESS

"Forgive? Are you kidding me? What she did to me is unforgivable!"

I get it! Truly, I do. I hated my own father for the first twenty-five years of my life for what he did to our family. He abused my mom, abandoned her, and left her to fend for herself. And he didn't stop with my mom—he went after my siblings and me too.

The difference between my siblings and me is that I was able, by the grace of God, to forgive him. Many of them did not. It's not that they explicitly refused to forgive him on purpose. Instead, it was that they just quit dealing with him. To them, he was just too much work, so they simply withdrew from him.

The problem with my siblings' approach is that withdrawing is not at all the same as forgiving. The virus of unforgiveness was still lingering in their minds and hearts, just waiting for another opportunity to destroy them all over again. The hurt? The pain? The trauma? All of that was still there; they just didn't talk about it anymore.

I'm not even sure they were aware that they were infected with the Singletary virus of unforgiveness, but I do know that simply not

---

10   "Beat Your Cravings: 8 Effective Techniques | Mayo Clinic Diet," Mayo Clinic, accessed April 23, 2025, https://diet.mayoclinic.org/us/blog/2021/beat-your-cravings-8-effective-techniques/.

PRINCIPLE 7: COMMITTED

knowing we are infected is not the same thing as not having the virus. Until we vaccinate against it, it's still there, ready to do its worst in our hearts and lives.

Forgiveness is an intentional act, one that must be engaged aggressively. It requires a head-on collision between our own will and the will of God.

Sometimes people tell me that they can't forgive, or that it would be wrong to forgive because letting their abuser off the hook would be the same as saying that what they did was OK. I always point out that forgiveness isn't about the person who wronged us. Most of us can walk and chew gum at the same time. I can condemn the trauma and abuse while letting go of my tendency to be responsible for what they did.

The reason that I believe this to be the healthiest approach is that while I'm letting my abuser live rent-free in my mind, they are going about their business without a care in the world. The only one who is suffering is me. I'm the one who is being eaten alive from the inside out. I am the one who is being overwhelmed by stress. I'm the one carrying the burden. It's my joy, my health, my relationships, and my life that are being stolen from me. Ironically, holding on to hatred and refusing to forgive is the best way to make sure that the person who wronged you gets off scot-free. No, that's wrong thinking.

We all reap what we sow. God will deal with them for what they did. I have to make sure what they did to me, intentionally or not, is between them and God. But I've got to deal with my unforgiveness. Unforgiveness will never punish the person who did me wrong. It punishes me.

And here's the worst part: Hurting people hurt other people. My own father is an example of this. I realized, almost too late, that he had an inner desire to be a better father than his dad had been, but

195

when he failed to forgive my grandfather, he carried the trauma into another generation. When I'm carrying around these resentments and hostilities, I can't help projecting all of that junk onto other people, often onto those closest to me. The cancer of unforgiveness gnaws on me from the inside out, eating me first and then the people I love.

That's why I had to forgive my dad. Unforgiveness had already stolen the best years of my siblings' lives, and it was beginning to devour mine too. I had to do it. It was my kryptonite, and I was no match for it.

If you're wondering how you can muster up the strength to forgive someone of even the most horrible wrongs, all I can tell you is that I began to think of how God had forgiven me of far greater guilt.

When someone does us wrong, they are only wronging another flawed human being. But my sin was a direct assault on the love of a perfect, holy, and sovereign God. The way I figured it then, and the way I figure it even now, is that if God could forgive me, I could forgive my dad.

Think about that. God offers forgiveness, but he doesn't ever say that the wrong I did to him was OK. In fact, he hated my sin so much that he sent his Son to die to pay for it. He paid for the wrong I did to him out of his own pocket. It cost him everything.

I'm glad he set me free from the responsibility of holding on to my resentments and unforgiveness so that I could love my wife and children in a way that my dad couldn't love his.

PERSISTENCE

I already told you about the day my dad left my mom, my sisters (Rudell and Mary), and me. What I haven't told you yet is that many of my mom's "advisors" told her that she should just apply for welfare and live off the government.

PRINCIPLE 7: COMMITTED

If anyone could make a case for doing that, she could have. With no formal education and no man in the house to bring home the bacon, what lay before her seemed like an impossible task.

That day is still a vivid memory for me. If I close my eyes and retrieve it from the back of my mind, I can still see my mother simultaneously sobbing and fervently praying. My heart truly broke for her because her fear was not theoretical; it was real. Her future looked impossibly bleak.

Finally, she dried her eyes and walked over to the telephone. Even to this day, I'm so proud to be Rudell Singletary's son because of what she did. Her first call was not to the welfare office but to businesses and friends that she thought might help her find a job. And when she was advised to just collect a welfare check, I recall her saying, "No! My God is bigger than this! He is greater than my circumstances."

It wasn't easy, especially at first. She began by babysitting other people's kids, but she finally got a job at a local hotel as a housekeeper. She often finished the day shift only to keep right on working through the night shift. I didn't count the number of nights she would come home from work only to fall asleep at the kitchen table, but it was a lot.

If you want to know what persistence means, my mother was the living definition. When the going got tough, she responded by saying, "I don't know how! I don't even know when! But I do know that somehow, some way, I'm going to accomplish this." She wasn't going to quit what she had started until she reached the finish line.

And here's the thing: The more she worked at being obedient to God by taking advantage of the opportunities he placed before her, the stronger she got. And the stronger she got, the stronger I got too.

Persistent people are infectious like that! The more we see them living in a way that says, "I won't give up! I will not quit! I will fight!"

5. COMMIT TO HELPING THOSE LOOKING FOR OPPORTUNITIES

I only met Cedric once, as far as I can remember. He was introduced to me by a business partner of mine who shared my passion for helping young people in poor neighborhoods find a way to be successful.

He and I had both noticed that many young, disadvantaged teens and young adults had never gotten a driver's license. For households making at least $100,000 per year, 86 percent of their children have either a driver's license or a learner's permit. But, only 57 percent of children whose families earn $50,000 or less have one.

This matters for a couple of reasons. One, not having a license makes getting a job, especially one that requires young people to drive, almost impossible. And two, when they do drive (and they often do despite not having a license), it makes them vulnerable to tickets and other traffic-related charges. Unfortunately, for kids whose culture has taught them to not trust the police, their first response to being pulled over by the cops is to floor it and run.

My partner had met Cedric in 2011 when he joined his table group at Prestonwood Baptist Church in Carrollton, Texas. Cedric had been led to the Lord by one of the youth ministers, who had been serving as a chaplain at Newman Smith High School.

A 325-pound offensive lineman at Newman Smith, he was a mountain of a kid. Still, as well as his enormous size, he possessed incredible wit and an infectious smile.

Cedric didn't have his own transportation, so the youth minister picked him up for youth activities. Later, my partner was recruited to swing by Cedric's house before the meetings and give him a ride.

PRINCIPLE 7: COMMITTED

It soon became apparent to him that Cedric had no real plan for getting his own license, much less ever getting his own car. So, he made a brief stop at the driver's license office and picked up a study manual for him. Cedric studied that thing relentlessly until he knew the material like he knew the back of his hand.

The day came for him to take his driving test. Unfortunately, Cedric panicked during the driving portion of the exam and ran a red light.

My friend began to work with Cedric for a few months, improving his confidence by teaching him to drive his car while my friend was in the passenger seat. When Cedric took the test again three months later, he passed with flying colors.

My friend said that Cedric's infectious smile grew into a wide grin when the examiner handed him his new license. He was beaming. He had accomplished something not many of his peers had.

Cedric began to work a few odd jobs over the following months and finally landed a job as an Amazon delivery driver. Not long after that, he found another job as a rescue driver and was eventually promoted to manager.

He bought his own car, rented an apartment, and took on a roommate. Not long after that, he was able to bring his daughter to his house on weekends so that he could remain involved in her life.

Cedric had been a kid who couldn't get out of his own way. He hadn't been a bad kid at all, but his family dynamics had made it seem impossible for him to get his own driver's license. Without mentors to guide him, he would have continued to flounder.

He was being raised by his grandmother, who herself had no skills. She had been stifled by her circumstances and couldn't grow. And because she was limited, Cedric was limited too. He could only

VISUALIZE YOUR GREATNESS

grow as far as she was able to grow. They both wanted to do better, but they had no idea how they could pull that off.

It was as if they felt victimized by being on the wrong channel but didn't even know it. Until they had someone to guide them in finding a better channel (like Norman Vincent Peale was for me), they would stay in the same place, listening to the same tired soap operas they'd always listened to.

I know how easy it is to look at the neighborhoods on the wrong side of the tracks and stigmatize everyone who lives there. It's a temptation for me to sometimes view people that way. But when I stop long enough to think about it, it's then that I realize, *those people* are me. I lived there.

So, on those occasions when I do put aside my prejudices long enough to think about it, I wonder, *How many kids like Mike Singletary are there in that neighborhood?*

That's not only a good question but a relevant one. Maybe if you'd seen me on your casual drive through Sunnyside back when I was a young boy, you might have been tempted to just write me off too. It would have been easy to do, to see me as just another Black boy from the ghetto.

What you couldn't have seen just passing by was that I had a desire, like a thirst that could not be quenched, to rise up out of the ashes of my circumstances and make something of myself. I wanted it, but I just didn't know how to do it until someone from somewhere else told me it was really possible.

How many Cedrics and Mike Singletarys are there in America's slums and poor rural communities, just hoping for a better life but not having any strategy for realizing it? There are a lot of them; I can tell you that.

PRINCIPLE 7: COMMITTED

Yes, I worked hard to get where I am. But I can tell you one thing: I didn't do it on my own. I had help. From my mom to Norman Vincent Peale to Coach Brown and a whole lot of other people (mainly men who cared enough about me to guide me into manhood), and I was able to make it.

If you are enjoying any measure of success, I can guarantee you that you had help too. Maybe it was your good fortune to have a mom and dad who guided you to where you are. From the moment of your birth, they laid the foundations for you that we have talked about in this book. Or maybe it was someone else. All I know is that none of us got where we are only through our own grit and determination. We all had guidance. We all had help.

So, the question is, how ungrateful is it for me to soak up all that was poured into me only to turn around and refuse to share what I've learned with kids who won't make it if I don't let them in on the secrets of success?

I've enjoyed it all—the accomplishments and the financial stability that have resulted from my days in the NFL. I can't imagine my life without my loving wife and seven incredible kids.

But I can tell you this too. Knowing kids like Cedric and playing a role in helping them get from where they came from to a better life has also been one of the greatest joys of my life.

6. COMMIT TO DOING IT TOGETHER

I don't know anyone who doesn't think that something's got to change if we are going to become a great nation again. But personally, I'm after more than that—I want to see us become greater than we've ever been before.

VISUALIZE YOUR GREATNESS

The problem with fruit like that is that it doesn't just fall off the trees by itself. The tree of success must be pruned and fertilized. We have to pay attention to its health and protect it from diseases and vermin that could destroy it or make it unfruitful.

One person can do a lot in the lives of a few people. But when we take a step back and look at the big picture of what is wrong in too many of our neighborhoods, we realize that it's too big for one person. There are just too many lost kids, kids like Cedric, who want better but don't know how to get it.

This is something that a lot of us are beginning to recognize: that we are more effective when we band together and launch a full-scale assault on the things that are holding back people who want better. When we join hands, we multiply our impact in communities across America.

Not only do we increase our effectiveness when we strategize and work together, but we learn from one another's mistakes and successes. When I hear that you've tried something that worked, I'll duplicate it in my efforts. When you find out that something I tried fell flat, you will avoid it.

And finally, our collective voice is louder. When we lobby politicians and other people in positions of power and influence, they can more easily hear what we are saying about, for example, vocational education and training. They can hear us when we advocate for healthcare and access to food for disadvantaged kids.

But even though I'm arguing for a collective effort, it still boils down to one person at a time taking up the mantle of being responsible for guiding these kids out of the mire. That person is me! I can't look at the big picture with any real sense of what needs to be done if I'm not seeing the Cedrics of America. These are kids who simply need someone older and more experienced to guide them out of the

202

PRINCIPLE 7: COMMITTED

shadows of America's incredible wealth and opportunity and into the light of prosperity.

So, I'm on my knees, praying for God to open my eyes so that I can see these kids—one at a time. In addition to that, I'm praying for him to empower me to see those young men and women in the same way he sees them: as objects of his divine love and affection. I'm pleading with him to give me the wisdom to mentor them by providing tested strategies for attaining success. And, finally, I'm praying for him to bring other people into my life who share this vision of helping these kids.

Yes, we are good individually, but when we are united in our desire to bring success to people who don't even know what that means, we are better together.

7. COMMIT TO YOURSELF

I committed to writing this book because of my vision for a better America, one where young people can see the incredible, limitless opportunities that are available to them. I am convinced that anyone can find success if they possess 1) a willingness to take sound advice from people who've done what they want to do, 2) a fierce spirit of determination to see their dreams come to fruition, and 3) a never-quit mentality.

I am committed to the big-picture change. But the big picture isn't changed all at once. It happens when enough individuals commit themselves to a better life and the hard work it takes to enjoy it in a way that overwhelms the culture of mediocrity and failure.

As you are wrapping up your reading of this book, that's what I hope you take away from it. It's just you and me in the room, and we've just spent the last few hours talking about success and how to

VISUALIZE YOUR GREATNESS

achieve it. If you walk away from our conversation and return to your old approach to life, then we failed to accomplish our mission.

But, first, you must be committed to yourself—not in a selfish way but committed to living in a way that is about more than you. The truly successful life is about us, all of us. It's about our communities, schools, churches, states, and nations. It's about how we fit into the solution for how we can all rise up and be what God intended for us to be.

It is success wrapped in noble character. Anything less is unattractive. Worse than that, it is an unfruitful life. Live your life in a way that others want to follow and emulate. We need leaders like you, leaders who are willing to give the world what it needs.

EPILOGUE

So, here we are at the finish line, as far as our conversation is concerned. Hopefully, you read this book with a mental picture of just you and me sitting across the table from one another, talking about success.

But before I let you go, I want to share one more thing with you to wrap up everything we've talked about. As it turns out, this one thing is the greatest secret in our world today. Wanna hear it? Well, here it is!

Greatness is in you!

Does this shock you? Do you "feel" like you are always falling short of what you wish you could be in life? When I tell you that greatness is in you, do you secretly tell yourself, "Yeah, that's easy for him to say. Mike doesn't know how many times I've fallen flat on my face in failure!"

Actually, I do understand!

So, let me share with you what I learned about life from playing sports as a kid. The good news is that it's really quite simple. Don't let the rest of the world complicate it for you because there are only three things you need to know in order to begin to fully realize your potential and become successful. That's right! Just three things to get you on the right road.

1. I HAVE TO BE IN THE PROPER ALIGNMENT

Am I where I'm supposed to be? Or am I just there because someone said I'm supposed to be there? Or did it just look like fun, so I thought I'd do it too? Or it looked like everyone else was doing it, so I thought I'd just join in because of my fear of missing out?

Well, I've heard those things before, and it's OK because no one wants to be alone. I get it! But I found that in order for me to be the best I could be in life, I needed to ask myself three questions about my alignment:

- First, am I where I believe that my time, my talents, and skills are best utilized?

- Second, do I believe that this is my calling in life? My purpose?

- And third, do I really love what I am pursuing?

This question about alignment is a very, very important one because if I'm in proper alignment, and if I believe that this is where I'm supposed to be, and if I truly love what I have committed to doing, then I have a chance to make a difference. Not only do I have a chance to make the play, but I give those around me a chance to make the play too because I'm where I'm supposed to be. When we are all properly aligned, we're all in the right spot. And there's no greater feeling on a team than to know that you are where you're supposed to be and so are your teammates.

But when I'm out of position, I put myself in danger of missing the play because I'm not where I'm supposed to be. And by being out of position, I will probably prevent my teammates from making the play too.

So, examine yourself to discover whether you are aligned properly. Are you certain, deep in your heart, that you are where you're supposed to be? Are you convinced that this is where God has gifted you to use your talents?

2. IF I AM IN THE PROPER ALIGNMENT, DO I HAVE MY ASSIGNMENT?

Once you answer yes to whether you are in the proper alignment, the next question is, "What is my assignment?" Am I doing the right thing?

When I first began to play organized football, most of the coaches, as well as my teammates, said, "Mike, you look like either a fullback or a strong safety. You would be perfect for one of those positions."

But when I asked what the purpose of those positions was, they explained, "Well, a fullback blocks for the running back most of the time, and the strong safety covers the tight ends or the fullback from the defensive side of the ball. Sometimes, he is close to the line of scrimmage, and sometimes he is not."

Nothing about either of those positions excited me. But when the coach mentioned playing middle linebacker, I asked him, "What does he do?" The coach said, "The middle linebacker is the lion of the defense. He's smart! He is mean and nasty! And he hits everything that moves. He sets the tempo for how the defense plays, starting with the huddle. He calls the plays, looking in the eyes of the players in the huddle to make sure they are ready to play. Then he leads by example in everything he does. He's the hardest working guy on the defense every day of the week—in practice, in the game, and even off the field. He knows what it's going to take to win, week in and week out. And he makes sure that, to the best of his ability, he does it. That's his job."

When I heard that, I knew right away. "That's who I am! That's me!" I knew deep in my heart that this was my position. All I needed to know was what my assignment was, and my assignment was to hit everything that moved. So, I had the right alignment, which was being in the right place to do my job, and then I had my assignment to do the right job.

3. I MUST USE THE RIGHT TECHNIQUE

In football, this takes using the right posture, leverage, and the correct foot and eye placement. The skills needed are vitally important. I don't mean just the talent we are born with; I mean the skills we develop when we don't just go through the motions and keep repeating the same mistakes. Instead, it's the skill we develop when we look honestly at our mistakes and ask ourselves, "What did I do wrong? What do I need to change to be able to do this well?"

I learned this while playing sports, but it's just as true in all areas of life, especially the areas in which we desire greatness. We can't just go through the motions in life, learning nothing from our experiences and mistakes. This takes a ton of repetition, doing it over and over and over again, but doing it with excellence every time until I become the standard of excellence in whatever I'm doing.

Hopefully, after reading this book, you will realize that greatness is calling you. Even if the call you hear is only a faint whisper, I want to ask you something: Will you answer the call?

It will take courage to answer and say, "Here I am!" But I believe that by putting these seven *C*'s into daily practice, you can get there, one *C* at a time.

- Courage

- Consciousness

- Consistency

- Confidence

EPILOGUE

- Character

- Compete

- Commitment

The Seven C's of Success! Begin to put them into practice—today! If you stumble and fall, get up and start all over again. Don't stop! Ever! Greatness is waiting on you!

Now, if you'll do me a favor, I would consider this an honor. Find a quiet place, turn out the lights, close your eyes, and open your mind to what is in your heart. Have the courage to see it, maybe for the first time.

Now! Let's do it! Over and over and over again until you begin to see it so clearly that you can reach out and grab it. A move like this is so bold, it takes courage to do it. Don't let someone else talk you out of it.

Do it now! Don't put it off another day! This is yours to have.

ACKNOWLEDGEMENTS

In the last four to five years, I've read all I could find about the mind, health, family, and love, thinking a lot about the family I grew up with. The hard times, the good times, the fun, the tragic—they were all the foundation for the man I am today. Those tough times make me appreciate the love we have in our family today.

For me, outside of my Lord and Savior, Jesus Christ, I owe everything to my mother.

Rudell Hurd Singletary poured everything she had into her family, and because I was the last of her children, I probably got more of her than my siblings. I was sickly for the first bit of my life, so her constant prayers and declarations strengthened me from within. Her belief in me and whatever I set my mind to do fueled me through every obstacle I faced. I believed her when she told me that greatness was in me and carried myself accordingly from that day until today.

My siblings—Charlie, Jerome, Dale, JoAnn, Willie, Linda, Grady, Louise, and Rudell—possessed more raw talent than most people I know. They were strong, smart, and funny. Those who have passed on I miss dearly. They loved their baby brother and helped shape me into who I am today.

VISUALIZE YOUR GREATNESS

As soon as I humbled myself and let the Lord address my need to forgive my dad, I was able to crack through his crusty shell to find me. I saw so much of myself in his attempts to do the right thing, in spite of himself and him not having a roadmap to the success he dreamed of. He was rudderless as a thirteen year old boy on his own, and I found a love and respect for all he was able to accomplish. His work ethic was like none other, and the fact that nearly everything he did was self-taught still impresses me to this day.

Norman Vincent Peale, who I never had the opportunity to meet, helped me visualize the greatness my mom's words instilled in me. He helped me make my dreams of becoming a great football player a reality in my mind before I ever put on a football uniform.

My teachers and coaches were somehow able to see greatness in me, despite my often-stubborn exterior. With my teachers, I was very coachable. I was hungry to learn, and some of the most impactful were Mrs. Singleton in third grade, Mrs. Ferris in sixth, and Dr. Ann Miller at Baylor University. My coaches had to dig through a little more rubble to find all I had in me, but Coach Miller, Coach Cunningham, and Coach Brown were able to. Then, as I matured a bit, Coach Teaff and Coach Nelson were both able to plant the seeds for a successful NFL career, where Coach Ryan, Coach Ditka, and Dave McGinness took it upon themselves to invest in me as a man and a football player.

In my most vulnerable and pivotal time of life, Pastor Bill Hybels taught me about a God of grace that I never knew. Pastors Gerald and Becky Watson walked hand in hand with Kim and me and charted the path toward being the husband, father, and man I had always dreamed of being, but had no idea how to become.

To start singling out teammates runs the risk of offending anyone unnamed. Every person I played alongside, every player I went against

ACKNOWLEDGEMENTS

in practice and in games left an indelible mark on me. Everyone contributed to my Hall of Fame career in their own way. But my teammates at Baylor, Frank Ditta, Dennis Gentry, and Tommy Tabor were the few I allowed myself to have fun with (I was overly serious at that point in my life). And we sure had fun. In Chicago, Todd Bell, Danny Rains, Shaun Gayle, Al Harris, Leslie Frazier, Jim Osborne, and Revie Sorey may never know what a relief they were for me. They were my respite from the days I thought Buddy Ryan was truly trying to kill me. They helped me stay focused, sometimes reminded me of the need to chill out, and always encouraged me. Their belief in me helped fuel me.

My gratitude to Gordon Dasher and his gift of eloquence runs deep. Then, passing the baton to Eric Eggers and the team at Forbes helped get this book across the finish line.

And I've saved the best for last: my family. My wife Kim, who has been my best friend since I met her in her freshman year at Baylor in 1978. She helped me peel back layers of hurt, anger, frustration, and woundedness because she believed there was a nugget of goodness in me. I appreciate her patience and resilience while I grew into the man I pictured as a young boy. Our seven kids—Kristen, Matt, Jill, Jaclyn, Brooke, Becky, and John—the original nine. Everything I dreamed of as a kid who could only imagine a happy home like the ones on TV, came true in the way God gives you more than your wildest imagination. I have loved watching their personalities develop into what they are today. They have chosen God-gifted mates and have blessed us with grandchildren who will take our family to new heights. I want them all to know: Greatness is in you!

And I owe everything I am to my Lord and Savior, Jesus Christ. Without Him, I have no chance.